Success
Learn and Practise

Maths
age 10-11 · level four

YEAR
6

PLEASE DO NOT WRITE IN THIS BOOK –
Use your own paper to work through the questions.
THANK YOU

Paul Broadbent

D0259594

Contents

Using and applying mathematics

Counting and understanding numbers

Knowing and using number facts

Calculating

Understanding shape

Measuring

Handling data

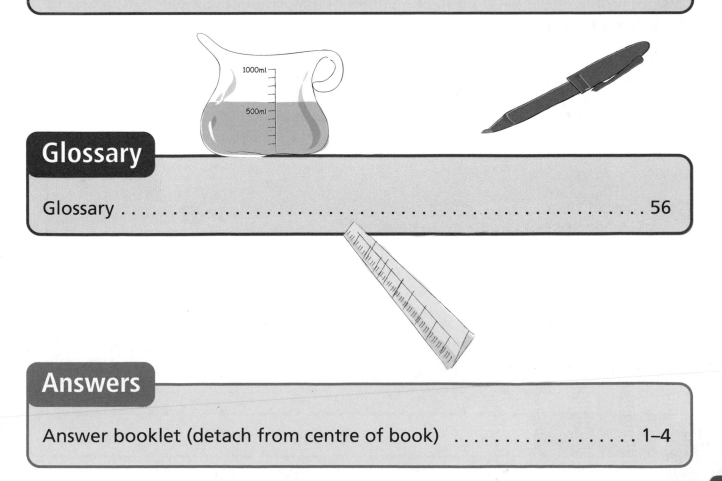

Glossary

Answers

Word problems

Answering problems

If you have a word problem to solve, it may help to follow these four stages.

Four tickets for a concert cost £58 altogether. What is the cost for three tickets?

1 Read the problem.
Try to picture the problem and imagine going through it in real life.

2 Sort out the calculations.
58 ÷ 4 will give the price of one ticket, then multiply the answer by 3 to find the cost of three tickets.

3 Answer the calculations.
58 ÷ 4 = 14.5
14.5 × 3 = 43.5

4 Answer the problem.
Look back at the question – what is it asking?
The cost for three tickets is £43.50.

 Top Tip *When you divide with money, you need a decimal answer rather than a remainder.*

Multi-step problems

Word problems can have different numbers of calculations to answer before you reach the final answer.

There are 26 boxes of light bulbs in a storeroom. There are 15 light bulbs in each box. How many light bulbs are there in total?

```
      26
×     15
     130
     260
=    390
```

There are 390 light bulbs altogether.

A square room has sides 8m long. A carpet costs £20 per square metre. What is the cost to carpet the whole room?

Step 1
Area of room is $8 \times 8 = 64m^2$.

Step 2
64 × 20 = 1280

Step 3
The carpet costs £1280.

Key words   remainder   area

4

Answering problems

1 A chef makes 340 sandwiches for a wedding. He has made 4 sandwiches per person. How many people are expected at the wedding?

85

2 It is 291km from Norwich to York. A bus travels there and back every day for 5 days. How far does the bus travel in total for these 5 days?

2910 km

3 A garden shed costs £487.35. It costs an extra £94.80 to have it delivered and put up. What will the total cost be?

£ **582.15**

4 Ali wants to raise £200 sponsorship by cleaning cars. He charges £6 to clean a car. What is the fewest number of cars he needs to clean to raise £200?

33

5 The cost of a holiday is £489 in March and £945 in August. What is the difference in cost between the two months?

£ **456**

6 Rebecca needs another 373 badges to have 2000 in her collection. How many badges does she have?

1627

6

Multi-step problems

1 In an office store there are 28 boxes of folders. Each box holds 36 folders, but one of the boxes has had 19 folders removed. How many folders are there in total?

989

2 A shirt costs £28 and a jumper costs £31. There is a 10% sale on these items. What will the total cost be in the sale?

£53·10

3 Josh uses 75g of flour, 40g of sugar and 53g of butter to make cookies. He divides the mixture equally to make 8 cookies. What is the weight of the mixture for each cookie?

21g

4 For 38 weeks of the year, a gardener works 8 hours a day for 5 days of the week. How many hours does he work in total for a year?

1520

5 A pack of six cartons of drink contains 942ml of drink in total. An individual can holds 168ml. Which holds more, a can or a carton?

a can

5

TOTAL MARKS 11

Problems and puzzles

Reasoning

If you need to think carefully about a way to solve a problem, you are likely to be using reasoning skills to make sense of it. Some maths questions look simple but involve a lot of thought. It may help to explain the problem to someone else, describing the way you could try to solve it.

I'm thinking of a number.

If I **double** it, the answer is 14 less than 40.

What is my number?

To answer this, work backwards through the problem.

14 less than 40 is 26. This is double the mystery number, so find half of 26.

The mystery number is 13.

Finding all possibilities

Some types of problems often have lots of different choices of answer and the skill is finding the correct one. You need to work systematically, making lists of all the possible answers to find the right one.

Robert's parcel cost £2.00 to post. He put 6 stamps on the parcel and each stamp was either 30p or 40p in value. How many of each stamp did he stick on his parcel?

Draw a table to help you answer this:

Number of stamps	30p stamps	40p stamps
1	30p	40p
2	60p	**80p**
3	90p	120p
4	**120p**	160p
5	150p	200p
6	180p	240p
7	210p	280p

Look for 6 stamps that total £2.00.

4 × 30p stamps and 2 × 40p stamps total £2.00.

Key words   double

Reasoning

1 I'm thinking of a number. If I halve the number and then add 8, the answer is 20. What number am I thinking of?

2 Sam bought three different coloured T-shirts. The white and black T-shirts cost a total of £14. The black and green T-shirts cost a total of £17. The white and green T-shirts cost a total of £15. What is the cost of each T-shirt?

Black T-shirt £ [ ]   White T-shirt £ [ ]   Green T-shirt £ [ ]

3 Ben's father was 33 when Ben was born. 8 years ago Ben's father was twice as old as Ben is now. How old is Ben?

4 These are the bills for three meals at a cafe.

| 1 cake |
| 1 coffee |
| Total: £1.70 |

| 2 cakes |
| 2 teas |
| Total: £3.20 |

| 1 tea |
| 2 coffees |
| Total: £2.30 |

What is the cost of each item?

1 cake = [ ] p   1 coffee = [ ] p   1 tea = [ ] p

4

Finding all possibilities

1 Which two square numbers total 100? _____

2 Ryan has some 20p and 10p coins. He has two more 10p coins than 20p coins and altogether he has £2.90. How many of each coin does he have? _____

3 **A** and **B** are two different whole numbers. **A + B = 121** **A** is 35 greater than **B**.

What are the numbers **A** and **B**?   **A** = _____   **B** = _____

4 Parveen buys some ice-creams and some lollies. Ice-creams cost £1.20 each and lollies cost 90p each. She buys three more ice-creams than lollies and spends exactly £12. How many of each does she buy?

_____ ice-creams   _____ lollies

4

Rules and patterns

Number sequences

A **sequence** is a list of numbers which usually have a pattern. You can often find the pattern or rule in a sequence by looking at the **difference** between the numbers.

What is the next number in this sequence?

39   35   31   27   _____

Each number is 4 less than the previous one, so the next number is 23.

Formulae and equations

A **formula** (plural is formulae) uses letters or words to give a rule.

Each table in a hall has 6 chairs around it.

How many chairs are needed for 8 tables? $6 \times 8 = 48$ chairs

How many chairs are needed for n tables? $6n$ chairs

Equations have symbols or letters instead of numbers in a calculation.

$\Delta + 2 = 15$

$? - 5 = 9$

$2y = 14$

You need to work out what the symbol or letter stands for. Use the numbers to help you and say it as a sentence. For example, What added to 2 makes 15?

$\Delta + 2 = 15$
$? - 5 = 9$
$2y = 14$

Top Tip *2y means y multiplied by 2. The × sign for multiplication isn't used in equations because it might look like a letter.*

Key words   sequence   difference   formula   equation

Number sequences

Write the missing numbers in these sequences.

1 [ ] 38 46 54 62 [ ]

2 95 [ ] [ ] 50 35 20

3 425 450 [ ] 500 [ ] 550

4 79 [ ] 71 [ ] 63 59

In these sequences each number is double the previous number. Write the missing numbers. You will need to use decimals for some sequences.

5 [ ] [ ] 8 16 32 [ ] [ ]

6 [ ] [ ] 44 88 176 [ ] [ ]

7 [ ] [ ] 10 20 40 [ ] [ ]

8 [ ] [ ] 30 60 120 [ ] [ ]

8

Formulae and equations

Write the value of each symbol or letter.

1 $16 + \triangle = 23$ $\triangle =$ [ ]

2 $? - 8 = 7$ $? =$ [ ]

3 $9\blacklozenge = 36$ $\blacklozenge =$ [ ]

4 $? \div 6 = 3$ $? =$ [ ]

5 $y + 22 = 38$ $y =$ [ ]

6 $40 - b = 15$ $b =$ [ ]

7 $7n = 35$ $n =$ [ ]

8 $27 \div t = 3$ $t =$ [ ]

8×9 $89 = 72$

Top Tip *If you're finding it difficult to work out the value of a letter, write it out again using a box instead of the letter. You can then try different numbers in the box to see if the equation works.*

8

TOTAL MARKS 16

Decimals

Decimal numbers

Decimal numbers are whole numbers divided into tenths, hundredths and thousandths. A decimal point is used to separate whole numbers from decimals.

Look at these number lines.

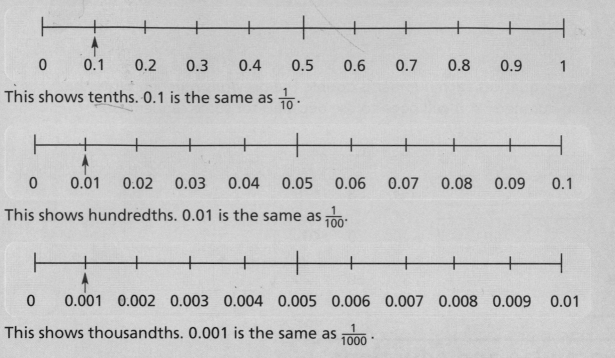

This shows tenths. 0.1 is the same as $\frac{1}{10}$.

This shows hundredths. 0.01 is the same as $\frac{1}{100}$.

This shows thousandths. 0.001 is the same as $\frac{1}{1000}$.

Multiplying and dividing by 10 and 100

To multiply by 10:
Move the digits one place to the left and fill the space with zero if needed.

$17.4 \times 10 = 174$
$238 \times 10 = 2380$

To multiply by 100:
Move the digits two places to the left and fill the spaces with zeros if needed.

$38.9 \times 100 = 3890$
$0.08 \times 100 = 8$

To divide by 10:
Move the digits one place to the right.

$17.8 \div 10 = 1.78$
$206 \div 10 = 20.6$

To divide by 100:
Move the digits two places to the right.

$49 \div 100 = 0.49$
$385 \div 100 = 3.85$

3.85 ÷ 100 = 385

Decimal numbers

Circle the fraction that is the same as each decimal number.

1	0.8	8	$\frac{8}{10}$	$\frac{8}{100}$	$\frac{8}{1000}$
2	0.007	7	$\frac{7}{10}$	$\frac{7}{100}$	$\frac{7}{1000}$
3	0.02	2	$\frac{2}{10}$	$\frac{2}{100}$	$\frac{2}{1000}$
4	0.63	63	$\frac{63}{10}$	$\frac{63}{100}$	$\frac{63}{1000}$
5	0.5	$\frac{1}{5}$	$\frac{1}{4}$	$\frac{1}{2}$	$\frac{3}{4}$
6	0.75	$\frac{1}{5}$	$\frac{1}{4}$	$\frac{1}{2}$	$\frac{3}{4}$

6

Multiplying and dividing by 10 and 100

Write the answers to these.

1 $0.9 \times 10 =$

2 $1.67 \times 10 =$

3 $5.02 \times 100 =$

4 $38.4 \times 100 =$

5 $13 \div 10 =$

6 $9.7 \div 10 =$

7 $405 \div 100 =$

8 $28 \div 100 =$

9 $21.5 \times 100 =$

10 $21.5 \div 100 =$

Top Tip *Putting a zero on the end of a decimal doesn't change the number. 1.2 is the same as 1.20 and 1.200.*

$0.9 \times 10 =$
$38.4 \times 100 =$
$28 \div 100 =$
$13 \div 10 =$
$9.7 \div 10 =$

10

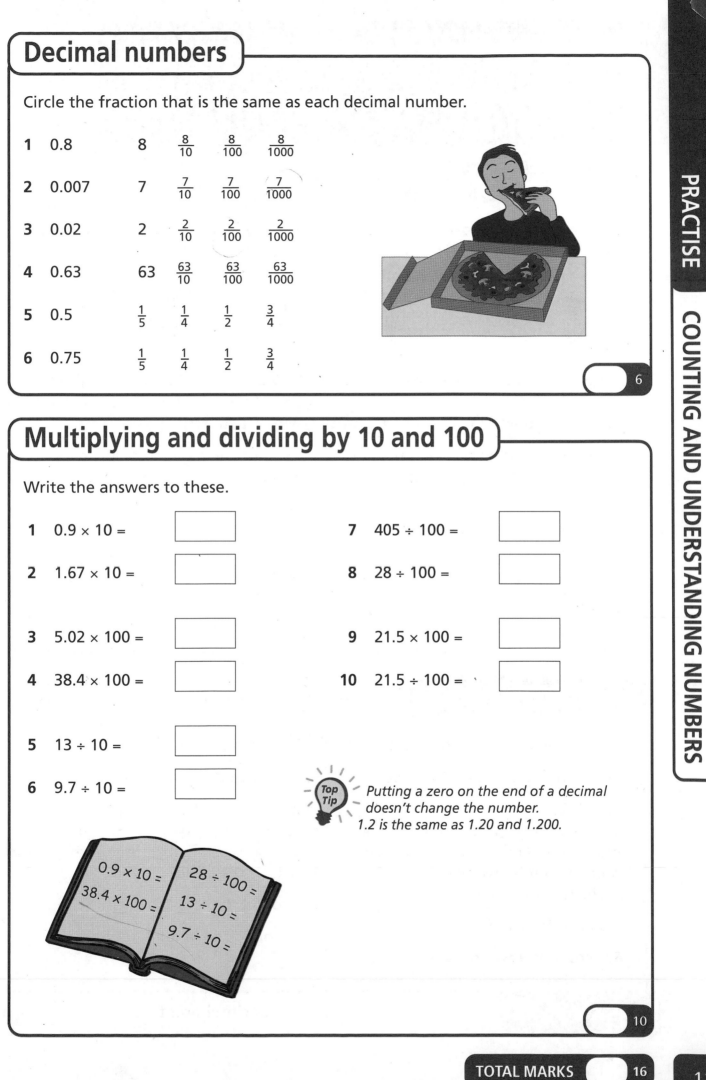

TOTAL MARKS 16

Ordering and rounding decimals

Ordering decimals

Putting decimals in order is just like putting whole numbers in order – you need to look carefully at the value of each **digit**.

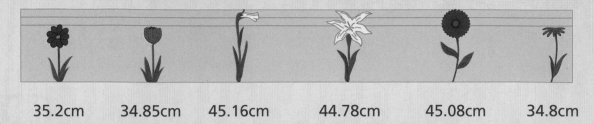

| 35.2cm | 34.85cm | 45.16cm | 44.78cm | 45.08cm | 34.8cm |

Write these flowers in order of size, starting with the tallest.

Write them out one under the other, lining up the **decimal points**.

35.2cm
34.85cm
45.16cm
44.78cm
45.08cm
34.8cm

Compare the digits from left to right and re-order the numbers.

45.16cm
45.08cm
44.78cm
35.2cm
34.85cm
34.8cm

Rounding decimals

Decimals are usually rounded to the nearest whole number or nearest tenth.

Rounding to the nearest whole number:

Look at the tenths digit. If it is 5 or more, round up to the next whole number. If it is less than 5, the units digit stays the same.

8.5 rounds up to 9.

3.46 rounds down to 3.

Rounding to the nearest tenth:

Look at the hundredths digit. If it is 5 or more, round up to the next tenth. If it is less than 5, the tenth digit stays the same.

6.76 rounds up to 6.8.

4.347 rounds down to 4.3.

Key words   digit   decimal point

Ordering decimals

Write each set of decimals in order in the boxes to make these correct.

1   4.7   7.4   7.7   4.4   [ ] < [ ] < [ ] < [ ]

2   29.1   12.9   19.2   9.2   [ ] > [ ] > [ ] > [ ]

3   3.58   5.83   5.38   8.35   [ ] > [ ] > [ ] > [ ]

4   2.46   19.23   2.09   19.18   [ ] < [ ] < [ ] < [ ]

5   6.06   60.6   60.66   60.06   [ ] < [ ] < [ ] < [ ]

6   5.1   15.51   15.5   5.15   [ ] > [ ] > [ ] > [ ]

Top Tip

< and > are symbols used to compare numbers.
*< means **is less than**. For example: 9.57 < 9.75*
*> means **is greater than**. For example: 0.9 > 0.78*

6

Rounding decimals

Round each amount to the nearest whole number.

1   27.6cm   ➔   [ ] cm   4   20.5g   ➔   [ ] g

2   5.92ml   ➔   [ ] ml   5   11.08km   ➔   [ ] km

3   £83.49   ➔   £ [ ]

Round each amount to the nearest tenth.

6   £7.07   ➔   £ [ ]

7   5.364 litres ➔   [ ] litres

8   15.51m   ➔   [ ] m

9   9.828kg   ➔   [ ] kg

10   42.339km ➔   [ ] km

£7.07 to the nearest tenth?

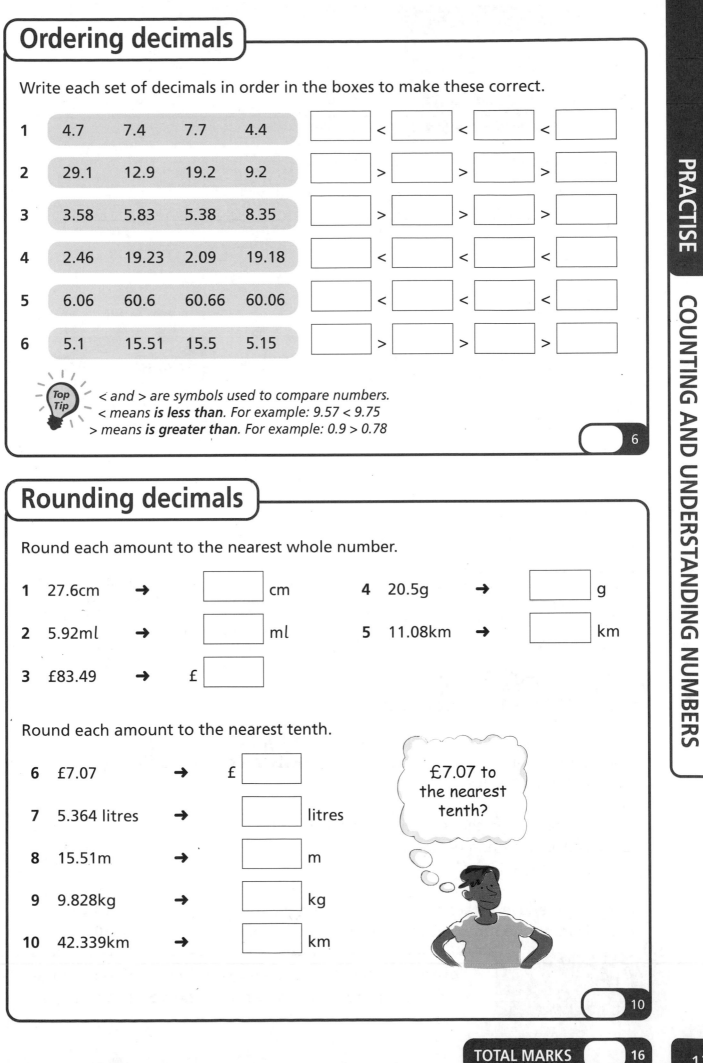

10

TOTAL MARKS [16]

Fractions

Types of fractions

Look at these three types of fractions.

1 A **proper fraction**, such as $\frac{2}{5}$, which is less than 1.

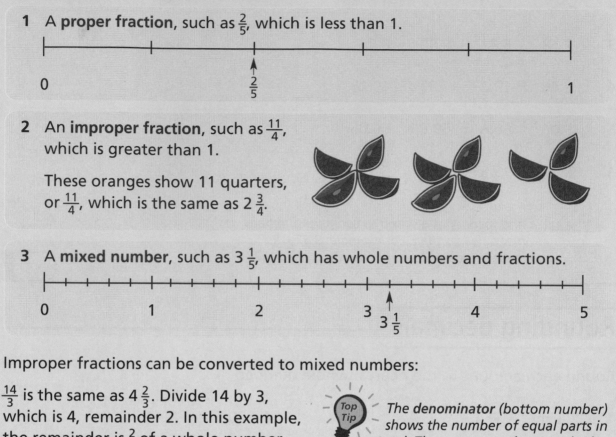

2 An **improper fraction**, such as $\frac{11}{4}$, which is greater than 1.

These oranges show 11 quarters, or $\frac{11}{4}$, which is the same as $2\frac{3}{4}$.

3 A **mixed number**, such as $3\frac{1}{5}$, which has whole numbers and fractions.

Improper fractions can be converted to mixed numbers:

$\frac{14}{3}$ is the same as $4\frac{2}{3}$. Divide 14 by 3, which is 4, remainder 2. In this example, the remainder is $\frac{2}{3}$ of a whole number.

Top Tip *The **denominator** (bottom number) shows the number of equal parts in total. The **numerator** (top number) shows how many equal parts are taken.*

Equivalent fractions

Equivalent fractions have different numerators and denominators but have the same value.

$\frac{2}{3}$ = $\frac{4}{6}$

A fraction can be changed into its equivalent by multiplying the numerator and denominator by the same amount.

$$\frac{3 \times 4 = 12}{4 \times 4 = 16}$$

You can reduce a fraction to an equivalent fraction by dividing the top and bottom by the same number.

$$\frac{40 \div 10 = 4}{50 \div 10 = 5}$$

Key words   proper fraction   improper fraction   mixed number
denominator   numerator   equivalent fractions

Types of fractions

Match each improper fraction to the mixed number which has the same value. One has been done for you.

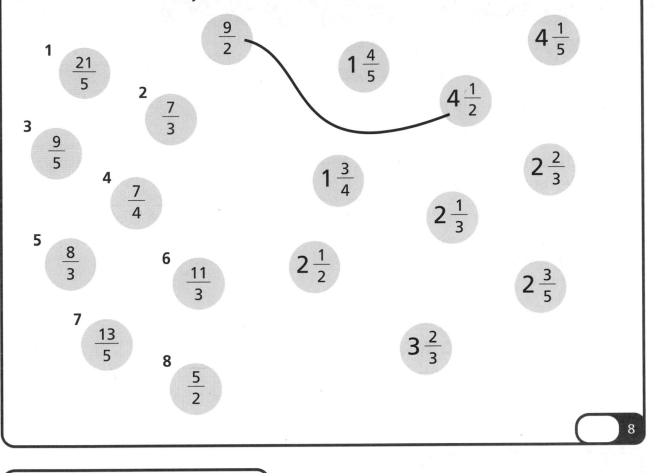

8

Equivalent fractions

Complete these equivalent fractions.

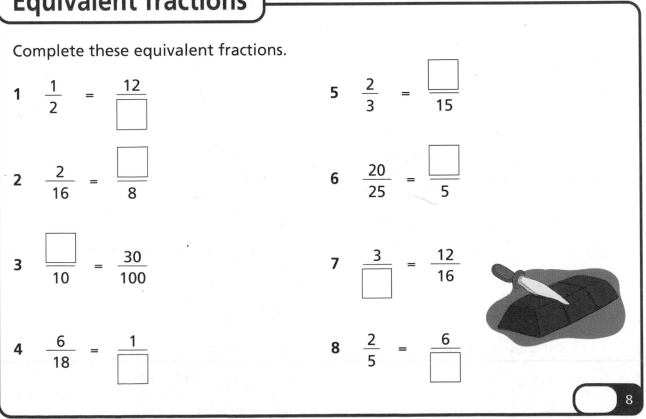

1   $\dfrac{1}{2}$ = $\dfrac{12}{\Box}$

2   $\dfrac{2}{16}$ = $\dfrac{\Box}{8}$

3   $\dfrac{\Box}{10}$ = $\dfrac{30}{100}$

4   $\dfrac{6}{18}$ = $\dfrac{1}{\Box}$

5   $\dfrac{2}{3}$ = $\dfrac{\Box}{15}$

6   $\dfrac{20}{25}$ = $\dfrac{\Box}{5}$

7   $\dfrac{3}{\Box}$ = $\dfrac{12}{16}$

8   $\dfrac{2}{5}$ = $\dfrac{6}{\Box}$

8

Fractions, decimals, percentages

Percentages and fractions

Percentages are simply fractions out of 100. That's what per cent means: out of 100. % is the percentage sign.

In a tile pattern of 100 square tiles, 40 are coloured red.

40% of the tiles are red.

Another tile pattern of 20 square tiles has 8 red tiles.

This also means 40% of the tiles are red.

To change fractions to percentages, make them out of 100. This means you need to find an equivalent fraction with the denominator 100.

$\frac{2}{5}$ is equivalent to $\frac{40}{100}$.

$\frac{2}{5} = 40\%$

To change per cent to fraction, write the percentage as a fraction out of 100 and then simplify.

25% is $\frac{25}{100}$, which is the same as $\frac{1}{4}$.

Equivalent values

Decimals	0.1	0.2	0.3	0.4	0.5	0.6	0.7	0.8	0.9	0.25	0.75
Fractions	$\frac{1}{10}$	$\frac{1}{5}$	$\frac{3}{10}$	$\frac{2}{5}$	$\frac{1}{2}$	$\frac{3}{5}$	$\frac{7}{10}$	$\frac{4}{5}$	$\frac{9}{10}$	$\frac{1}{4}$	$\frac{3}{4}$
Per cent	10%	20%	30%	40%	50%	60%	70%	80%	90%	25%	75%

Percentages and decimals

Converting between percentages and decimals is easy.

Per cent to decimal:

Divide the percentage by 100.

60% is the same as 0.6.

35% is the same as 0.35.

Decimal to per cent:

Multiply the decimal by 100.

0.7 is the same as 70%.

0.25 is the same as 25%.

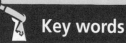 **Key words**   percentage

Percentages and fractions

Change these maths test scores to percentages.

1 Leah $\frac{7}{10}$ → [   ] %

2 Ryan $\frac{15}{20}$ → [   ] %

3 Josh $\frac{4}{5}$ → [   ] %

4 Gita $\frac{33}{50}$ → [   ] %

5 Beth $\frac{15}{25}$ → [   ] %

6 Which child has the highest percentage score? _____

Top Tip *If you find it easier, write the fraction as a decimal and then multiply by 100. $\frac{3}{4}$ is 0.75, which is the same as 75%.*

[6]

Equivalent values

Read and answer these questions.

1 What is nought point eight as a percentage? [   ] %

2 Write twenty per cent as a decimal. [   ]

3 What is three quarters as a decimal? [   ]

4 What is half as a percentage? [   ] %

[4]

Percentages and decimals

Write the missing percentage or decimal to complete this table.

0.3		0.94	0.05		
	60%			1%	26%

[6]

TOTAL MARKS [16]

Number facts

Multiplication and division facts

Here are all the multiplication and division facts to 100. Cover up different numbers in the grid and say the hidden numbers as quickly as possible.

×	1	2	3	4	5	6	7	8	9	10
1	1	2	3	4	5	6	7	8	9	10
2	2	4	6	8	10	12	14	16	18	20
3	3	6	9	12	15	18	21	24	27	30
4	4	8	12	16	20	24	28	32	36	40
5	5	10	15	20	25	30	35	40	45	50
6	6	12	18	24	30	36	42	48	54	60
7	7	14	21	28	35	42	49	56	63	70
8	8	16	24	32	40	48	56	64	72	80
9	9	18	27	36	45	54	63	72	81	90
10	10	20	30	40	50	60	70	80	90	100

$9 \times 3 = 27$ $27 \div 3 = 9$

$3 \times 9 = 27$ $27 \div 9 = 3$

Top Tip Remember that 3×8 gives the same answer as 8×3, so you only have to learn half the facts.

These are the facts that cause the most problems:

3×8 4×7 4×8 4×9 6×7
6×8 7×8 9×6 7×9 8×9

Learn one fact a day – it will only take 10 days! Try this: every time you go through a doorway at home, say the fact out loud. You'll soon know it off by heart.

Square numbers

The numbers in the green squares above are square numbers.

$1 \times 1 = 1$ $2 \times 2 = 4$ $3 \times 3 = 9$ $4 \times 4 = 16$ $5 \times 5 = 25$

$6 \times 6 = 36$ $7 \times 7 = 49$ $8 \times 8 = 64$ $9 \times 9 = 81$ $10 \times 10 = 100$

Learn these special numbers. Why do you think they are called square numbers?

Key words   square number

Multiplication and division facts

1 $9 \times 7 = \boxed{63}$

2 $15 \div 3 = \boxed{05}$

3 $7 \times 6 = \boxed{42}$

4 $36 \div 9 = \boxed{04}$

5 $8 \times 4 = \boxed{32}$

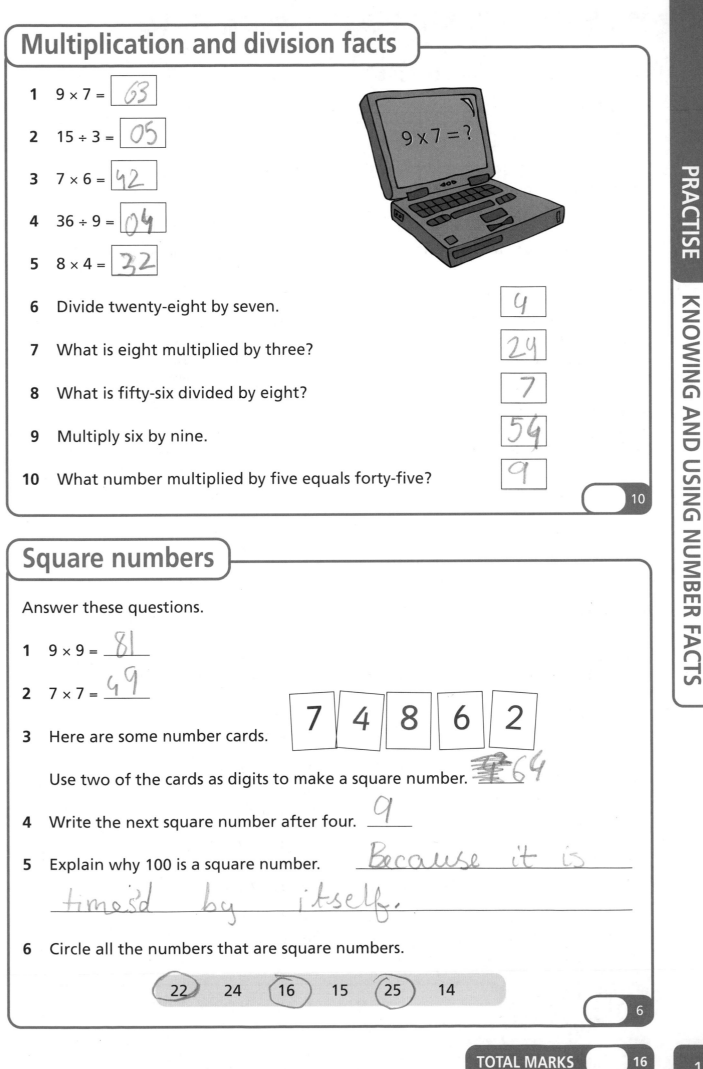

$9 \times 7 = ?$

6 Divide twenty-eight by seven. $\boxed{4}$

7 What is eight multiplied by three? $\boxed{24}$

8 What is fifty-six divided by eight? $\boxed{7}$

9 Multiply six by nine. $\boxed{54}$

10 What number multiplied by five equals forty-five? $\boxed{9}$

10

Square numbers

Answer these questions.

1 $9 \times 9 = \underline{81}$

2 $7 \times 7 = \underline{49}$

3 Here are some number cards. $\boxed{7} \boxed{4} \boxed{8} \boxed{6} \boxed{2}$

Use two of the cards as digits to make a square number. ~~4~~ 64

4 Write the next square number after four. $\underline{9}$

5 Explain why 100 is a square number. <u>Because it is</u> <u>times'd by itself.</u>

6 Circle all the numbers that are square numbers.

(22)   24   (16)   15   (25)   14

6

TOTAL MARKS 16

Multiples and factors

Factors

Factors are numbers that will divide exactly into other numbers. It is useful to put factors of numbers into pairs.

| Factors of 21 | ➤ | (1, 21), (3, 7) | 21 has 4 factors. |
| Factors of 18 | ➤ | (1, 18), (2, 9), (3, 6) | 18 has 6 factors. |

Did you know that numbers always have an even number of factors, unless it is a square number? Try it – how many factors has 16 or 25 got?

Top Tip A *prime number* only has two factors, 1 and itself. For example, 23 is a prime number as it can only be divided exactly by 1 and 23.

Multiples

A multiple is a number made by multiplying together two other numbers. So the multiples of:

2 are 2, 4, 6, 8, 10 … and so on.   3 are 3, 6, 9, 12, 15 … and so on.

Rules of divisibility

These are rules to test whether a number is a multiple of 2, 3, 4, 5, 6, 8, 9 and 10. A whole number can be divided by:

2, if the last digit is even.
56, 204, 4350

3, if the sum of its digits can be divided by 3.
435
(4 + 3 + 5 = 12),
3840
(3 + 8 + 4 + 0 = 15)

4, if the last two digits can be divided by 4.
184, 740, 2364

5, if the last digit is 0 or 5.
920, 175, 6085

6, if it is even and divisible by 3.
828, 504, 126

8, if half of the number is divisible by 4.
240, 112, 328, 488

9, if the sum of its digits is divisible by 9.
495, 108, 585, 270

10, if the last digit is 0.
760, 980, 370, 160

Key words   factor   prime number   multiple

Nikita Nikita   16/5/18

Factors

1 Circle the numbers that are **not** factors of 24.

1   2   3   4   5   6   7   8   9

(5, 7, 8, 9 circled; 8 crossed out with 8 written above)

1, 32

2 Write the missing factors for 32.

(1, 32) (1 , 32) (8 , 4)

3 Write a factor of 30 that is greater than 12.   ~~___~~ 30x1

4 Write the factors for 49 in order, starting with the smallest.

1, 49, 7, 7,

4

Multiples

Write each of these four numbers in the correct place on this Venn diagram.

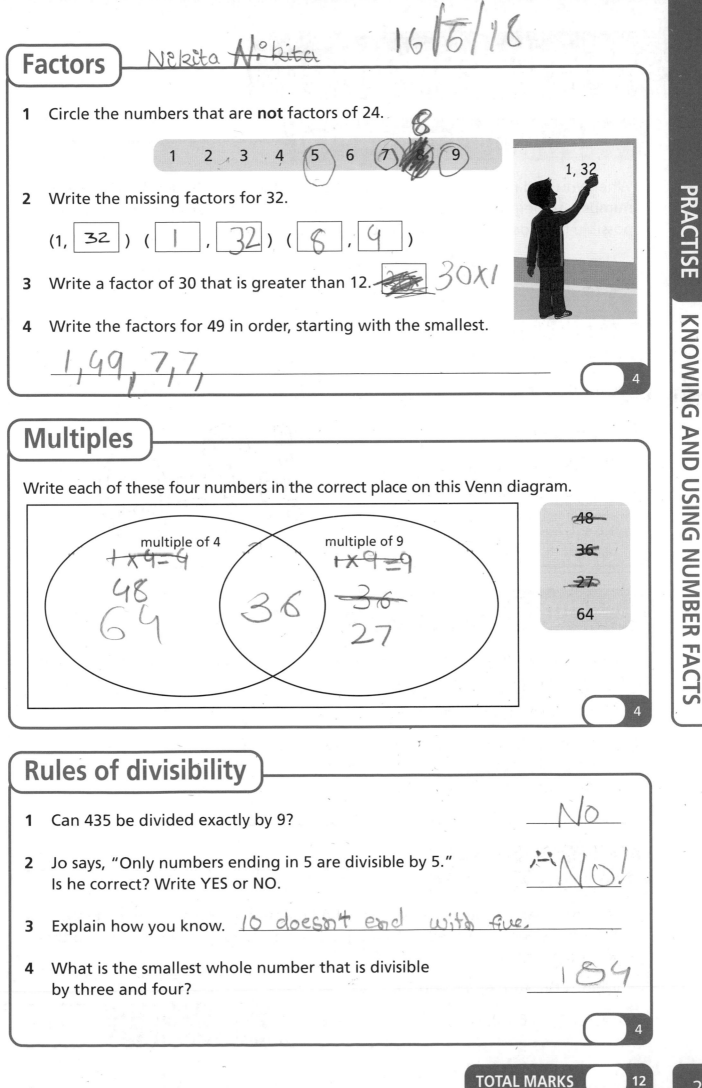

multiple of 4

1x4=4
48
64

36

multiple of 9

1x9=9
~~36~~
27

48
36
27
64

4

Rules of divisibility

1 Can 435 be divided exactly by 9?   No

2 Jo says, "Only numbers ending in 5 are divisible by 5."
Is he correct? Write YES or NO.   No!

3 Explain how you know.   10 doesn't end with five.

4 What is the smallest whole number that is divisible
by three and four?   184

4

TOTAL MARKS   12

Mental addition

Mental methods for addition

When you add numbers in your head, the first thing you should do is look at the numbers to help you choose the best method to find the answer. These are a few possible methods, but choose the one that works for you.

Use patterns:

$6 + 7 = 13$

$86 + 7 = 93$

$60 + 70 = 130$

$0.6 + 0.7 = 1.3$

Use rounding:

$37 + 9 \rightarrow 37 + 10 - 1 = 46$

$23 + 19 \rightarrow 23 + 20 - 1 = 42$

$2.5 + 3.9 \rightarrow 2.5 + 4 - 0.1 = 6.4$

Use near doubles:

$18 + 19 = 18 + 18 + 1 = 37$

$25 + 26 = 25 + 25 + 1 = 51$

$1.6 + 1.7 = 1.6 + 1.6 + 0.1 = 3.3$

Adding 2-digit numbers

If you need to add two big numbers in your head, it helps to break the numbers up and add the tens, then the ones.

$85 + 57$ Use these three steps:

1   Hold the bigger number in your head: 85.
2   Break 57 into $50 + 7$. Add the tens: $85 + 50 = 135$.
3   Add the ones: $135 + 7 = 142$.

Adding decimals

To add decimals in your head, you may find it easier to add the whole numbers, then add the tenths. If the tenths total more than 1, you just add 1 more to the whole number total.

What is the **sum** of 4.6 and 3.8?

$4 + 3 = 7$ $0.6 + 0.8 = 1.4$ So, $7 + 1.4 = 8.4$

Key words   sum

Mental methods for addition

Choose a mental method and write the answers to these.

1   What number is nineteen more than fifty-seven?   `76`

2   In Year 5 there are two classes. One has 28 pupils,
    the other has 27. How many children are there in
    the year in total?   `55`

3   Add together sixty and ninety.   `150`

4   A bus has 34 passengers and another 17 get on the bus.
    How many passengers are there altogether on the bus now?   `51`

5   What is the total weight of two cakes
    weighing 2.5kg and 2.6kg?   `5.1` kg

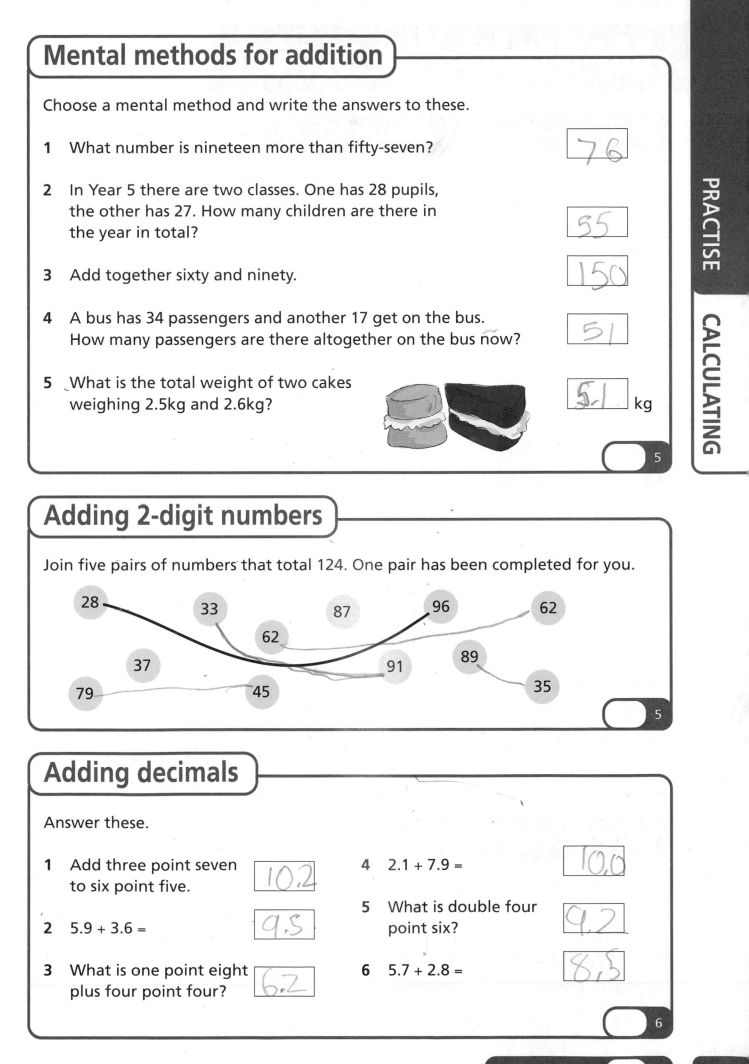

5

Adding 2-digit numbers

Join five pairs of numbers that total 124. One pair has been completed for you.

28   33   87   96   62
      62
  37   91   89
79   45   35

5

Adding decimals

Answer these.

1   Add three point seven
    to six point five.   `10.2`

2   5.9 + 3.6 =   `9.5`

3   What is one point eight
    plus four point four?   `6.2`

4   2.1 + 7.9 =   `10.0`

5   What is double four
    point six?   `9.2`

6   5.7 + 2.8 =   `8.5`

6

TOTAL MARKS   16

Mental subtraction

Mental methods for subtraction

When you subtract numbers in your head, look at the numbers to help you choose the best method to find the answer. Here are some possible methods, but choose the one that works for you.

Use patterns:

$13 - 8 = 5$

$53 - 8 = 45$

$130 - 80 = 50$

$1.3 - 0.8 = 0.5$

Use rounding:

$24 - 9 \rightarrow 24 - 10 + 1 = 15$

$35 - 19 \rightarrow 35 - 20 + 1 = 16$

$6.5 - 3.9 \rightarrow 6.5 - 4 + 0.1 = 2.6$

Use inverses:

$25 - \square = 18$

$18 + 7 = 25$

So $25 - 7 = 18$

Counting on

A really good method for a take-away or subtraction is to find the difference between the numbers by counting on.

What is the difference between 38 and 64?

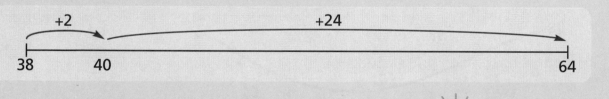

This number line shows exactly what goes on in your head.

Count on from 38 to 40. Hold the 2 in your head.

40 to 64 is 24.   24 + 2 is 26.   So $64 - 38 = 26$

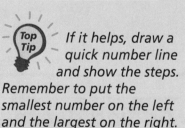

Top Tip *If it helps, draw a quick number line and show the steps. Remember to put the smallest number on the left and the largest on the right.*

Subtracting decimals

To subtract decimals in your head, try counting on from the smaller decimal to the next whole number and then counting on to the larger decimal.

Subtract 3.8 from 7.4. → 3.8 on to 4 is 0.2 (hold that in your head).
→ 4 on to 7.4 is 3.4. → 3.4 added to 0.2 is 3.6.

$7.4 - 3.8 = 3.6$

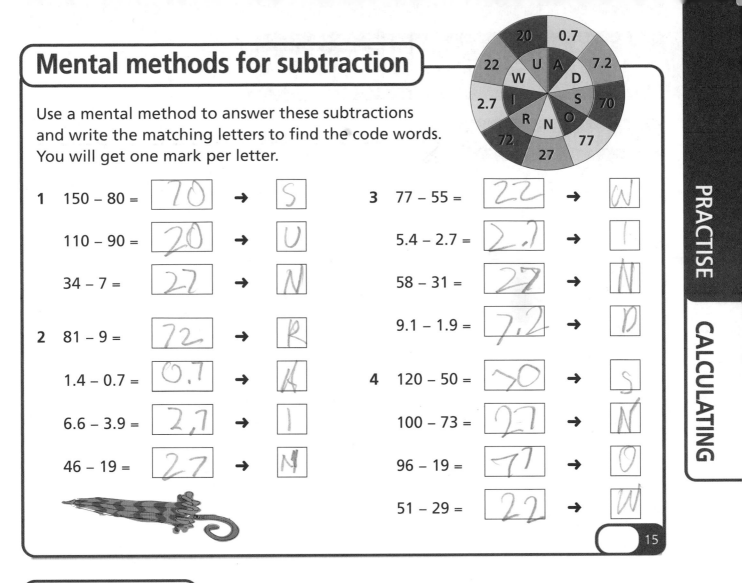

Mental methods for subtraction

Use a mental method to answer these subtractions and write the matching letters to find the code words. You will get one mark per letter.

1 150 – 80 = $\boxed{70}$ → $\boxed{S}$

110 – 90 = $\boxed{20}$ → $\boxed{U}$

34 – 7 = $\boxed{27}$ → $\boxed{N}$

2 81 – 9 = $\boxed{72}$ → $\boxed{R}$

1.4 – 0.7 = $\boxed{0.7}$ → $\boxed{A}$

6.6 – 3.9 = $\boxed{2.7}$ → $\boxed{I}$

46 – 19 = $\boxed{27}$ → $\boxed{N}$

3 77 – 55 = $\boxed{22}$ → $\boxed{W}$

5.4 – 2.7 = $\boxed{2.7}$ → $\boxed{I}$

58 – 31 = $\boxed{27}$ → $\boxed{N}$

9.1 – 1.9 = $\boxed{7.2}$ → $\boxed{D}$

4 120 – 50 = $\boxed{70}$ → $\boxed{S}$

100 – 73 = $\boxed{27}$ → $\boxed{N}$

96 – 19 = $\boxed{77}$ → $\boxed{O}$

51 – 29 = $\boxed{22}$ → $\boxed{W}$

15

Counting on

Write the five missing numbers on this difference grid.

	53	17	84
25		8	
96	43		12
60		43	

5

Subtracting decimals

Use these numbers to answer the following: 8.3   2.4   4.9   7.5   5.6

1 Which two numbers have a difference of 3.2? $\boxed{8.3}$ $\boxed{7.5}$

2 Which number is 4.6 less than 9.5? $\boxed{4.9}$

3 Which two numbers have a difference of 0.8? $\boxed{5.6}$ $\boxed{4.9}$

4 What is the answer if you subtract the smallest number from the greatest number? $\boxed{5.9}$

4

TOTAL MARKS   24

Written addition

Written addition

When you add numbers using this written method, make sure you line up the **columns** carefully.

What is 3492 added to 2631?

Step 1

$2 + 1 = 3$

```
   3492
 + 2631
      3
```

Step 2

$90 + 30 = 120$

```
   3492
 + 2631
     23
    1
```

Top Tip — Write the sum neatly to keep the columns in line. Mistakes can be made if you squash it all together.

Step 3

$100 + 400 + 600 = 1100$

```
   3492
 + 2631
    123
   1 1
```

Step 4

$1000 + 3000 + 2000 = 6000$

```
   3492
 + 2631
   6123
   1 1
```

Adding decimals

When you add decimals, remember to line up the **decimal points**. The method is the same as with whole numbers.

What is the total of 17.9, 3.8 and 8.64?

1 Write them in a column, lining up the decimal points.

2 Start by adding from the right-hand column.

3 Keep going left until all the columns have been added.

```
   1 7 . 9
     3 . 8
 +   8 . 6 4
   3 0 . 3 4
   2 2
```

Key words column   decimal point

Written addition

Write in the missing numbers to complete these additions.

1
```
    4 6 1 [9]
  +  3 [6] 4 8
  _____
    8 2 6 7
```

2
```
    2 1 [1] 5
  +  5 4 1 [6]
  _____
    7 5 3 1
```

3
```
    1 8 4 9
  +  3 6 6 [4]
  _____
    5 5 [1] 3
```

4
```
    4 [2] 9 4
  +  3 . 7 [8] 6
  _____
    8 0 8 0
```

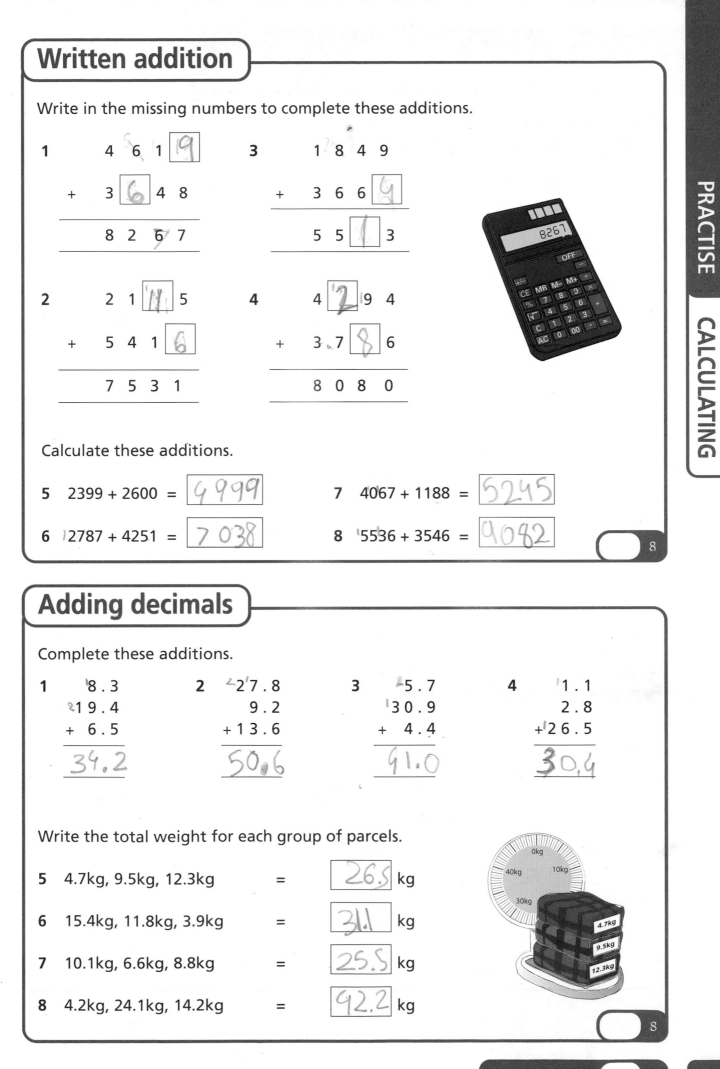

Calculate these additions.

5   2399 + 2600 = `4999`

6   2787 + 4251 = `7038`

7   4067 + 1188 = `5245`

8   5536 + 3546 = `9082`

8

Adding decimals

Complete these additions.

1
```
   8 . 3
  19 . 4
 + 6 . 5
 _____
  34.2
```

2
```
  27 . 8
   9 . 2
 +13 . 6
 _____
  50.6
```

3
```
   5 . 7
  30 . 9
 + 4 . 4
 _____
  91.0
```

4
```
   1 . 1
   2 . 8
 +26 . 5
 _____
  30.4
```

Write the total weight for each group of parcels.

5   4.7kg, 9.5kg, 12.3kg   =   `26.5` kg

6   15.4kg, 11.8kg, 3.9kg   =   `31.1` kg

7   10.1kg, 6.6kg, 8.8kg   =   `25.5` kg

8   4.2kg, 24.1kg, 14.2kg   =   `92.2` kg

8

TOTAL MARKS   16

Written subtraction

Written subtraction

If you can't work out a subtraction in your head, this is one method you can try.

What is 3674 subtract 1738?

Step 1

Rename 70 + 4 as 60 + 14.

14 − 8 = 6

$$3\,6\,6\,7\,4$$
$$-\ \ 1\,7\,3\,8$$
$$\overline{\hphantom{0000}6}$$

Step 2

60 − 30 = 30.

$$3\,6\,6\,7\,4$$
$$-\ \ 1\,7\,3\,8$$
$$\overline{\hphantom{0000}3\,6}$$

Top Tip **Important!** Remember to always take the bottom number away from the top number.

Step 3

Rename 3000 + 600 as 2000 + 1600
1600 − 700 = 900.

$$^2 3^1 6^6 7^4$$
$$-\ \ 1\,7\,3\,8$$
$$\overline{\hphantom{000}9\,3\,6}$$

Step 4

2000 − 1000 = 1000.

$$^2 3^1 6^6 7^4$$
$$-\ \ 1\,7\,3\,8$$
$$\overline{\hphantom{00}1\,9\,3\,6}$$

Number line method

Another written method to try uses a number line to find the difference between the numbers by counting on.

What is the difference between 126.8 and 173?

1   Draw a blank number line from 126.8 to 173.

2   Count on to 127, then to 130 and then to 173 to find the difference:

+0.2   +3   +43

126.8 127   130   173

3   Add up all the jumps.   0.2 + 3 + 43 = 46.2

So the difference between 126.8 and 173 is 46.2.

Written subtraction

Complete these subtractions.

1	8 3 9 1	2	4 5 1 0 6	3	6 7 3 2	4	8 5 4 4
	− 7 1 5 7		− 3 8 7 2		− 5 3 7 8		− 7 2 9 8
	1239		1234		1354		1245

Calculate the answers to these subtractions.

5   What is 8391 subtract 3719? ☐ 4672

6   What is the difference between 3846 and 7203? ☐ 3267

7   Which number is 2948 less than 6149? ☐ 3201

8   What is 4006 minus 1557? ☐ 559

8

Number line method

Use a number line to find the difference between each pair of numbers.

1   56.9 ——————————— 94   ☐ 37.1

2   119.5 ——————————— 182   ☐ 625

3   35.3 ——————————— 77.6   ☐ 42.3

4   143.9 ——————————— 162.7   ☐ 18.8

Calculate these subtractions.

5   185 − 126.4 =   ☐ 58.6 ~~10.4~~

6   374 − 309.8 =   ☐ 64.2

7   96.2 − 55.9 =   ☐ 40.3

8   171.5 − 139.7 =   ☐ 31.8

374 − 309.8 = ?

8

TOTAL MARKS ☐ 16

Multiplication

Mental calculations

Use times tables to help to multiply 2-digit numbers by a single digit in your head.

What is 53 multiplied by 4?

Use these three steps:

1 Multiply the tens: 50 × 4 = 200.

2 Multiply the units: 3 × 4 = 12.

3 Add the two parts: 200 + 12 = 212.

53 × 4

Column method

This is a written method for multiplying 2-digit numbers.

What is 47 multiplied by 23?

Top Tip *With all multiplications, always estimate an approximate answer first. 47 x 23 is approximately 50 x 20, so the answer should be close to 1000.*

```
    47        →   leading to  →        47
  ×  23                              ×  23
   800    (40 × 20)                   940    (47 × 20)
   140    (7 × 20)                     141    (47 × 3)
   120    (40 × 3)                    1081
    21    (7 × 3)
  1081
```

Grid method

For this method, the numbers are broken up into tens and units and written in a grid. Multiply each pair of numbers to complete the grid and add up each row to find the total.

×	40	7
20	800	140
3	120	21

→ 940

→ 141

Total: 1081

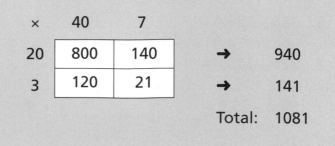

🔑 **Key words**   estimate   approximate

Answers

PAGE 5

Answering problems
1 85   4 34
2 2910km   5 £456
3 £582.15   6 1627

Multi-step problems
1 989   4 1520
2 £53.10   5 a can
3 21g

PAGE 7

Reasoning
1 24
2 Black T-shirt ➜ £8   White T-shirt ➜ £6
   Green T-shirt ➜ £9
3 25 years old
4 1 cake = 90p   1 coffee = 80p
   1 tea = 70p

Finding all possibilities
1 36 and 64
2 nine 20p coins and eleven 10p coins
3 A = 78   B = 43
4 7 ice-creams   4 lollies

PAGE 9

Number sequences
1 **30**   38   46   54   62   **70**
2 95   **80**   **65**   50   35   20
3 425   450   **475**   500   **525**   550
4 79   **75**   71   **67**   63   59
5 2   4   8   16   32   **64**   **128**
6 **11**   **22**   44   88   176   **352**   **704**
7 **2.5**   **5**   10   20   40   **80**   **160**
8 **7.5**   **15**   30   60   120   **240**   **480**

Formulae and equations
1 $\triangle = 7$ 5 $y = 16$
2 $? = 15$ 6 $b = 25$
3 $\blacklozenge = 4$ 7 $n = 5$
4 $? = 18$ 8 $t = 9$

PAGE 11

Decimal numbers
1 $\frac{8}{10}$ 4 $\frac{63}{100}$
2 $\frac{7}{1000}$ 5 $\frac{1}{2}$
3 $\frac{2}{100}$ 6 $\frac{3}{4}$

Multiplying and dividing by 10 and 100
1 9   6 0.97
2 16.7   7 4.05
3 502   8 0.28
4 3840   9 2150
5 1.3   10 0.215

PAGE 13

Ordering decimals
1 4.4   <   4.7   <   7.4   <   7.7
2 29.1   >   19.2   >   12.9   >   9.2
3 8.35   >   5.83   >   5.38   >   3.58
4 2.09   <   2.46   <   19.18   <   19.23
5 6.06   <   60.06   <   60.6   <   60.66
6 15.51   >   15.5   >   5.15   >   5.1

Rounding decimals
1 28cm   6 £7.10
2 6ml   7 5.4 litres
3 £83.00   8 15.5m
4 21g   9 9.8kg
5 11km   10 42.3km

PAGE 15

Types of fractions
1 $\frac{21}{5}$ ➜ $4\frac{1}{5}$ 5 $\frac{8}{3}$ ➜ $2\frac{2}{3}$
2 $\frac{7}{3}$ ➜ $2\frac{1}{3}$ 6 $\frac{11}{3}$ ➜ $3\frac{2}{3}$
3 $\frac{9}{5}$ ➜ $1\frac{4}{5}$ 7 $\frac{13}{5}$ ➜ $2\frac{3}{5}$
4 $\frac{7}{4}$ ➜ $1\frac{3}{4}$ 8 $\frac{5}{2}$ ➜ $2\frac{1}{2}$

Equivalent fractions
1 $\frac{1}{2} = \frac{12}{24}$ 5 $\frac{2}{3} = \frac{10}{15}$
2 $\frac{2}{16} = \frac{1}{8}$ 6 $\frac{20}{25} = \frac{4}{5}$
3 $\frac{3}{10} = \frac{30}{100}$ 7 $\frac{3}{4} = \frac{12}{16}$
4 $\frac{6}{18} = \frac{1}{3}$ 8 $\frac{2}{5} = \frac{6}{15}$

PAGE 17

Percentages and fractions
1 70%   4 66%
2 75%   5 60%
3 80%   6 Josh

Equivalent values
1 80%   3 0.75
2 0.2   4 50%

Percentages and decimals

0.3	**0.6**	0.94	0.05	**0.01**	**0.26**
30%	60%	**94%**	5%	1%	26%

PAGE 19

Multiplication and division facts
1 63   6 4
2 5   7 24
3 42   8 7
4 4   9 54
5 32   10 9

Square numbers
1 81
2 49
3 64
4 9
5 10 multiplied by itself is 100.
6 16, 25

PAGE 21
Factors
1 5, 7, 9
2 (1, 32) (2, 16) (4, 8)
3 15 or 30
4 1, 7, 49

Multiples

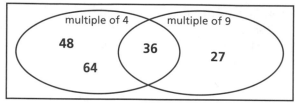

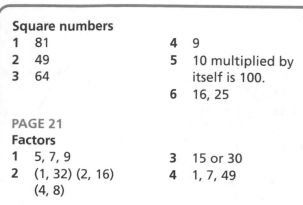

Rules of divisibility
1 No
2 No
3 10, 20 and other numbers ending with zero can also be divided by 5.
4 12

PAGE 23
Mental methods for addition
1 76
2 55
3 150
4 51
5 5.1kg

Adding 2-digit numbers
33 → 91
62 → 62
79 → 45
37 → 87
89 → 35

Adding decimals
1 10.2
2 9.5
3 6.2
4 10
5 9.2
6 8.5

PAGE 25
Mental methods for subtraction
1 70 → S
   20 → U
   27 → N
2 72 → R
   0.7 → A
   2.7 → I
   27 → N
3 22 → W
   2.7 → I
   27 → N
   7.2 → D
4 70 → S
   27 → N
   77 → O
   22 → W

Counting on

	53	17	84
25	28	8	59
96	43	79	12
60	7	43	24

Subtracting decimals
1 2.4 and 5.6
2 4.9
3 8.3 and 7.5
4 5.9

PAGE 27
Written addition
1
```
    4 6 1 9
  + 3 6 4 8
    8 2 6 7
```
2
```
    2 1 1 5
  + 5 4 1 6
    7 5 3 1
```
3
```
    1 8 4 9
  + 3 6 6 4
    5 5 1 3
```
4
```
    4 2 9 4
  + 3 7 8 6
    8 0 8 0
```
5 4999
6 7038
7 5255
8 9082

Adding decimals
1 34.2
2 50.6
3 41
4 30.4
5 26.5kg
6 31.1kg
7 25.5kg
8 42.5kg

PAGE 29
Written subtraction
1 1234
2 1234
3 1354
4 1246
5 4672
6 3357
7 3201
8 2449

Number line method
1 37.1
2 62.5
3 42.3
4 18.8
5 58.6
6 64.2
7 40.3
8 31.8

PAGE 31
Mental calculations

1. 1	■	2. 3	3	3. 5	■	4. 2
5. 1	9	0	■	6. 1	8	4
4	■	7. 8	3	0	■	5

Column method
Check the method and each answer.
1 910
2 1596
3 2736
4 2116

Grid method
Check the method and each answer.
1 1426
2 2862

PAGE 33
Written methods
Check the method and each answer.
1 162
2 65 r 2
3 276 r 1
4 52 r 3
5 51 r 3
6 292
7 88 r 4
8 230

Remainder problems
1   7 packs
2   8 bunches
3   2 packs
4   14 panels
5   9 weeks
6   14 full egg boxes
7   7 packs
8   17 2kg bags

PAGE 35
Fractions and division
1   20
2   15
3   4
4   60
5   12
6   30

Numerator greater than 1
1   6, 12
2   4, 12
3   3, 6
4   2, 10
5   £9
6   16 girls
7   80 metres
8   30
9   20

PAGE 37
Percentages of a quantity

	10%	20%	5%	50%	25%
£20	£2	£4	£1	£10	£5
£60	£6	£12	£3	£30	£15
£50	£5	£10	£2.50	£25	£12.50

Discounts and sale prices
1   £36
2   £81
3   £27
4   £63
5   £72
6   £9

PAGE 39
Lines of symmetry

1
1 line of symmetry

2
0 lines of symmetry

3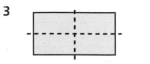
2 lines of symmetry

4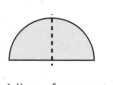
1 line of symmetry

5
3 lines of symmetry

6
4 lines of symmetry

7
5 lines of symmetry

8
6 lines of symmetry

Reflections

1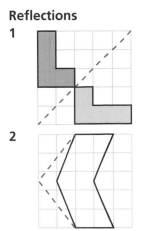

2

3

4

PAGE 41
Triangles

1

2

3

4

5   60°
6   Yes

Quadrilaterals
1   rectangle
2   kite
3   square
4   True
5   False
6   True

PAGE 43
Properties of 3D shapes

Shape	Number of flat faces	Number of vertices	Number of edges
Sphere	0	0	0
Cuboid	6	8	12
Triangular prism	5	6	9
Tetrahedron	4	4	6
Cylinder	2	0	2
Square-based pyramid	5	5	8

Nets of solids

1

2   Any one of the following squares shaded.

3 and 4

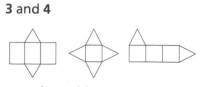

red   blue

PAGE 45
Positions on a grid
1	gate	5	(1,5)
2	bridge	6	(8,2)
3	stables	7	(3,8)
4	tree	8	(6,4)

Shapes and coordinates
1	(4,4)	3	(5,10)
2	(6,9)	4	(0,5)

PAGE 47
Types of angles
Number of:	right angles	obtuse angles	acute angles	reflex angles
Shape A	2	1	1	0
Shape B	1	2	1	0
Shape C	0	0	3	0
Shape D	0	0	3	1

Measuring angles
1	130°	3	30°
2	105°	4	280°

Angles and shapes
1	50°	3	75°
2	60°	4	20°

PAGE 49
Units of measure
1   80ml, 180ml, 1.8 litres, 18 litres
2   3.5mm, 30mm, 3.5cm, 350cm
3   50g, 250g, $\frac{1}{2}$ kg, 1.2kg
4   600ml, 6 litres, 6600ml, 60 litres

Converting units
1	400ml or 0.4l	3	10 jugs
2	1.75m, 175cm, or 1m 75cm	4	95cm or 0.95m

Reading scales
1	Jug A	3	1.2kg
2	850ml	4	Check that arrow is pointing to 1.2kg.

PAGE 51
Perimeter of rectangles
1	29cm	3	36m
2	44cm	4	176m

Finding areas
1	2 squares	3	6 squares
2	10 squares	4	5.5 squares

Area of rectangles
1	127.5m^2	2	400cm^2	3	14cm

PAGE 53
24-hour time

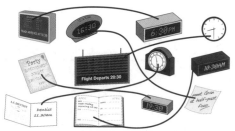

Calculating times
1	10.10am	3	50 minutes
2	19.55	4	4.13

Appleby	09.35	11.50	**14.02**	16.38
Berrytown	09.58	12.13	14.25	**17.01**
Limewich	**11.00**	13.15	15.27	**18.03**
Pearham	11.39	**13.54**	**16.06**	18.42

PAGE 55
Bar charts
1	16	5	10
2	sparrow	6	finches
3	9	7	94
4	pigeons		

Frequency charts and grouped data
1	under 2km	4	4–6km
2	9	5	18
3	9		

Letts Educational
4 Grosvenor Place, London SW1X 7DL
Orders: 015395 64910
Enquiries: 015395 65921
Email: enquiries@lettsandlonsdale.co.uk
Website: www.lettsandlonsdale.com

First published 2009

Editorial and design: 2ibooks [publishing solutions] Cambridge
Author: Paul Broadbent
Book concept and development: Helen Jacobs, Publishing Director
Editorial: Sophie London, Senior Commissioning Editor
     Katy Knight, Junior Editor
Illustrators: Andy Roberts and Phillip Burrows
Cover design: Angela English

Every effort has been made to trace copyright holders and obtain their permission for the use of copyright material. The authors and publishers will gladly receive information enabling them to rectify any error or omission in subsequent editions. All facts are correct at time of going to press.

All our Rights Reserved. No part of the publication may be produced, stored in a retrieval system, or transmitted, in any form or by any means, electronic, mechanical, photocopying, recording or otherwise, without the prior permission of Letts Educational Ltd.

British Library Cataloging in Publication Data. A CIP record of this book is available from the British Library.

ISBN 9781844192182

Text, design and illustration © 2008 Letts Educational Ltd

Printed in Dubai

Letts Educational makes every effort to ensure that all paper used in its books is made from wood pulp obtained from well-managed forests, controlled sources and recycled wood or fibre.

Mental calculations

Answer these multiplications and complete the number puzzle.

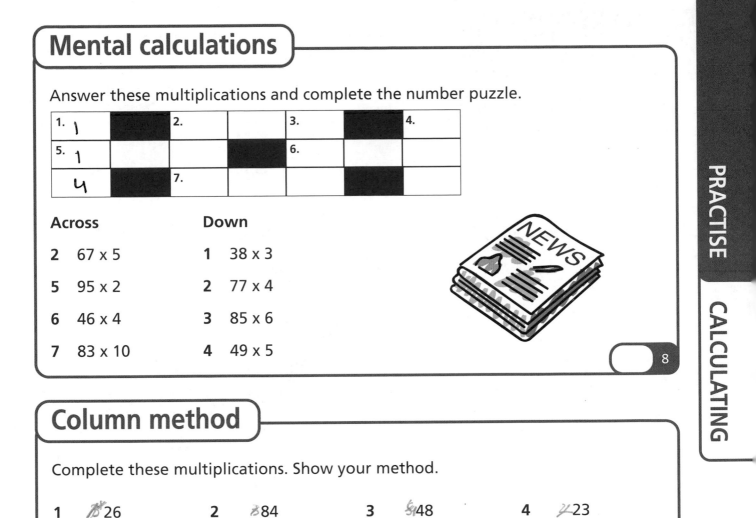

1. 1	■	2.		3.	■	4.
5. 1			■	6.		
4	■	7.			■	

Across

2   67 × 5

5   95 × 2

6   46 × 4

7   83 × 10

Down

1   38 × 3

2   77 × 4

3   85 × 6

4   49 × 5

8

Column method

Complete these multiplications. Show your method.

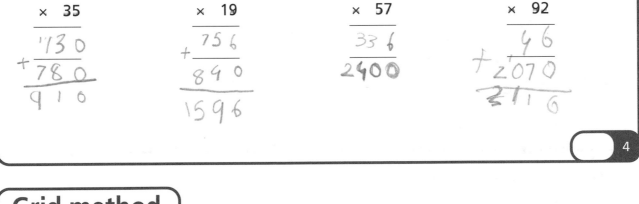

1
```
    26
  × 35
  ─────
   130
 + 780
  ─────
   910
```

2
```
    84
  × 19
  ─────
   756
 + 840
  ─────
  1596
```

3
```
    48
  × 57
  ─────
   336
  2400
```

4
```
    23
  × 92
  ─────
    46
 +2070
  ─────
  2116
```

4

Grid method

Complete these multiplications. Show your method.

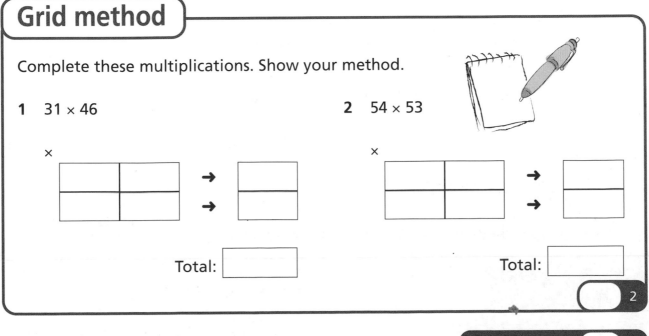

1   31 × 46

×

➜

➜

Total:

2   54 × 53

×

➜

➜

Total:

2

Division

Written methods

Before you start on a written division, work out an approximate answer first.

What is 789 divided by 4?

789 ÷ 4 is approximately 800 ÷ 4, so the answer will be less than 200.

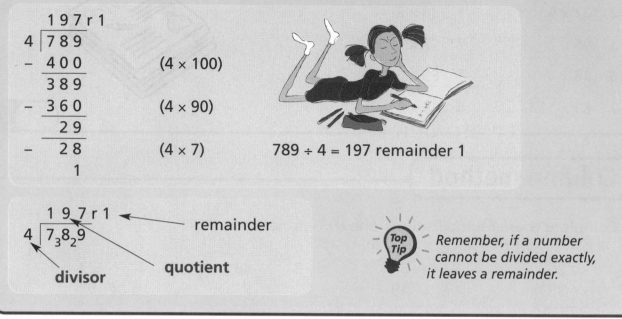

```
        1 9 7 r 1
    4 | 7 8 9
      -   4 0 0        (4 × 100)
          3 8 9
      -   3 6 0        (4 × 90)
            2 9
      -     2 8        (4 × 7)
              1
```

789 ÷ 4 = 197 remainder 1

```
        1 9 7 r 1  ←── remainder
    4 | 7₃8₂9
```
divisor   quotient

Top Tip Remember, if a number cannot be divided exactly, it leaves a remainder.

Remainder problems

When you have a division problem with a remainder, you need to decide what to do with the remainder. Should you round up the answer or round down?

Round up

54 people attend a dinner. The room has tables in it, with 4 people seated at each table. How many tables are needed in total?

54 ÷ 4 is 13 remainder 2, so 14 tables are needed.

Round down

I have £54. How many £4 posters could I buy for that amount?

54 ÷ 4 is 13 remainder 2, so 13 posters could be bought.

Key words   divisor   quotient

Written methods

Calculate the answer for each of these divisions. Show your method. You may need to use a separate piece of paper.

1 4) 6 4 8

2 3) 1 9 7

3 2) 5 5 3

4 4) 2 1 1

5 6) 3 0 9

6 3) 8 7 6

7 5) 4 4 4

8 4) 9 2 0

Top Tip *Division is the inverse or opposite of multiplication. So if you know your tables, it will really help you to divide numbers. What is 63 divided by 9? 9 x 7 = 63   63 ÷ 9 = 7*

8

Remainder problems

Answer these questions.

1 The school breakfast club needs 53 sausages. There are 8 sausages in a pack. How many packs are needed so that there are enough sausages?

2 Flowers are sold in bunches of 9. How many complete bunches can be made from 74 flowers?

3 A dog eats three chews a day. There are 12 chews in a pack. How many packs are needed for a week?

4 Fence panels are 3m wide. The distance round a garden is 40m. How many fence panels will be needed to put a fence the whole way round the garden?

5 Mr Jones wants to save £7 a week to buy a new garden chair at £59. How many weeks will it be before he can buy the chair?

6 A farmer collects 85 eggs in one day. How many egg boxes can he fill if each box holds 6 eggs?

7 Liam has a £15 gift voucher. How many £2 packs of stickers can he buy?

8 How many 2kg bags can be filled from a 35kg sack of rice?

8

TOTAL MARKS   16

Fractions of quantities

Fractions and division

Finding fractions of quantities is very similar to dividing amounts.

Look at these examples. What is…

$\frac{1}{3}$ of 15?

$\frac{1}{4}$ of 20?

These have 1 as a numerator, so simply divide by the denominator.

$\frac{1}{3}$ of 15 is $15 \div 3 = 5$.

$\frac{1}{4}$ of 20 is $20 \div 4 = 5$.

Numerator greater than 1

$\frac{1}{3}$ of 15 = 5.

This is easy, because we just divide by the denominator and count one of the groups.

$\frac{2}{3}$ of 15 = 10.

Now the numerator is 2, it means we count two of the groups.

If the numerator is more than 1, divide by the denominator and then multiply by the numerator. Look at these examples.

$\frac{2}{3}$ of 12 is $12 \div 3 = 4$, then $\times 2 = 8$.

$\frac{3}{5}$ of 25 is $25 \div 5 = 5$, then $\times 3 = 15$.

$\frac{3}{4}$ of 24 is $24 \div 4 = 6$, then $\times 3 = 18$.

$\frac{2}{3}$ of 12 is $12 \div 3 = 4$ then $\times 2 = 8$

Fractions and division

Write the missing numbers to make each of these correct.

1   $\frac{1}{2}$ of 10 = $\frac{1}{4}$ of ☐   4 $\frac{1}{3}$ of 18 = $\frac{1}{10}$ of ☐

2   $\frac{1}{4}$ of 12 = $\frac{1}{5}$ of ☐   5 $\frac{1}{6}$ of 24 = $\frac{1}{3}$ of ☐

3   $\frac{1}{10}$ of 20 = $\frac{1}{2}$ of ☐   6 $\frac{1}{5}$ of 25 = $\frac{1}{6}$ of ☐

6

Numerator greater than 1

Complete these sums.

1   ★★★★★★ ★★★★★★ ★★★★★★

$\frac{1}{3}$ of 18 is ☐ $\frac{2}{3}$ of 18 is ☐

2   ★★★★ ★★★★ ★★★★ ★★★★

$\frac{1}{4}$ of 16 is ☐ $\frac{3}{4}$ of 16 is ☐

3   ★★★ ★★★ ★★★ ★★★ ★★★

$\frac{1}{5}$ of 15 is ☐ $\frac{2}{5}$ of 15 is ☐

4   ★★ ★★ ★★ ★★ ★★ ★★

$\frac{1}{6}$ of 12 is ☐ $\frac{5}{6}$ of 12 is ☐

Answer these questions.

5   What is three-quarters of twelve pounds?   £ ☐

6   There are twenty-four children in a class and two-thirds are girls. How many are girls?   ☐

7   What is four-fifths of one hundred metres?   ☐ m

8   One third of a number is ten. What is the number?   ☐

9   Three-quarters of a number is fifteen. What is the number?   ☐

9

TOTAL MARKS ☐ 15

Percentages of quantities

Percentages of a quantity

What is 20% of £30?

There are several methods you could use to solve this type of **percentage** question.

Top Tip To find 5%, remember that it is half of 10%.

Method 1

Change to a fraction and work it out.

$20\% = \frac{20}{100} = \frac{1}{5}$

$\frac{1}{5}$ of £30 = £30 ÷ 5 = £6

Method 2

Use 10% to work it out – just divide the number by 10.

10% of £30 is £3.

So, 20% of £30 is double that: £6.

Method 3

If you are allowed, use a calculator to work it out.

Key in
20 ÷ 100 × 30 = _____

Discounts and sale prices

If you know how to work out percentages of amounts, you can work out sale prices.

A tennis racket costs £40. If there is 10% off, what is the sale price?

There are 2 steps to remember:

Step 1

Work out the percentage:

10% of £40 is £4.

Step 2

Take away this amount from the price:

£40 – £4 = £36

So the sale price is £36.

Key words   percentage

LEARN

CALCULATING

Percentages of a quantity

Fill in the ten missing amounts to complete this table, by working out the percentages of the amounts on the left.

	10%	20%	5%	50%	25%
£20			£1	£10	
£60	£6				
£50		£10			£12.50

10

Discounts and sale prices

In a sale everything is reduced by 10%. Write the cost of each item.

1 WAS £40   now 10% off

Sale Price: £ [   ]

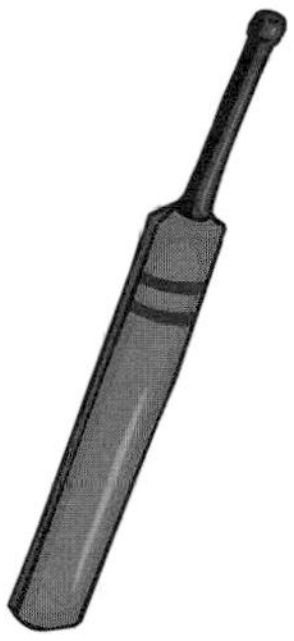

2 £90   LESS 10%

Sale Price: £ [   ]

3 WAS £30   10% discount today

Sale Price: £ [   ]

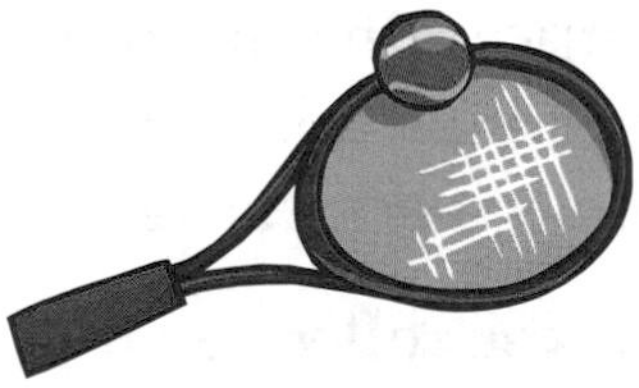

4 £70   SPECIAL OFFER 10% OFF

Sale Price: £ [   ]

5 WAS £80   now reduced by 10%

Sale Price: £ [   ]

6 £10   Bargain – SAVE 10% NOW

Sale Price: £ [   ]

6

TOTAL MARKS [   ] 16

Symmetry

Lines of symmetry

Some shapes are **symmetrical** – they have lines of symmetry, or reflective symmetry. Look at this shape.

If you imagine it folded down the middle, the two sides would look exactly the same. That fold line is the line of symmetry and shows if a shape or pattern is symmetrical.

Some shapes have more than one line of symmetry or no lines of symmetry:

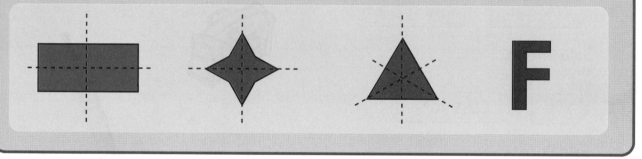

Reflections

You may be asked to draw the reflection of a picture or pattern, so that it is symmetrical. The mirror line is always drawn to help you, and the shapes are usually drawn on a grid. Use the squares on the grid to help you work out the position of each corner of the shape.

Draw the reflection of this shape.

Imagine the line is a mirror. Draw dots on each corner and count the squares across so that each point is reflected.

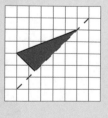

Top Tip *When a mirror is put on the line of symmetry, the half shape and its reflection show the whole shape. Practise using a small mirror to help you find symmetrical shapes.*

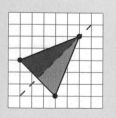

Key words   symmetrical

38

Lines of symmetry

Draw all the lines of symmetry on these shapes and write the number of lines of symmetry.

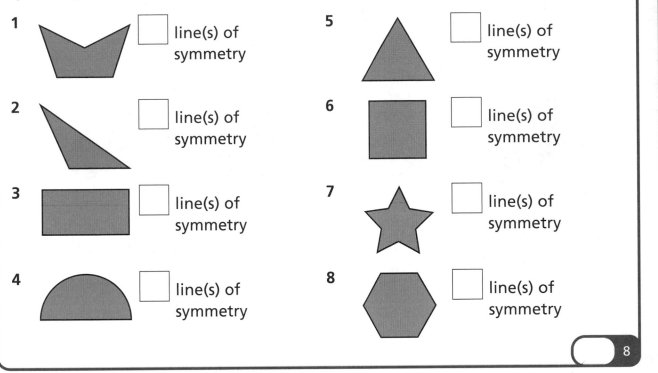

1   [ ] line(s) of symmetry

2   [ ] line(s) of symmetry

3   [ ] line(s) of symmetry

4   [ ] line(s) of symmetry

5   [ ] line(s) of symmetry

6   [ ] line(s) of symmetry

7   [ ] line(s) of symmetry

8   [ ] line(s) of symmetry

8

Reflections

Complete these questions.

1   Shade more squares to make a reflection on the mirror line.

2   Here is part of a shape. Draw two more lines to make a shape with a line of symmetry. Use a ruler.

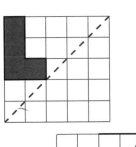

3   Draw a reflection of this shape. Use a ruler.

4   Shade more squares so that the design is symmetrical in both mirror lines.

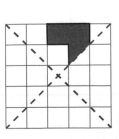

4

2D shapes

Triangles

Look at the properties of these different triangles.

| **Equilateral**
3 equal sides.
3 equal angles. | **Isosceles**
2 equal sides.
2 equal angles. | **Right-angled**
One angle is a
right angle. | **Scalene**
No equal sides.
No equal angles. |

Quadrilaterals

These are some special four-sided shapes.

| **Square**
4 equal sides.
4 equal angles. | **Rectangle**
2 pairs of equal sides.
4 right angles. | **Rhombus**
4 equal sides.
Opposite angles equal.
Opposite sides **parallel**. |
| **Parallelogram**
Opposite sides are equal
and parallel. | **Kite**
Two pairs of **adjacent**
sides are equal. | **Trapezium**
One pair of parallel sides. |

🔑 **Key words** | parallel adjacent

Triangles

Here are four regular hexagons.
Join three dots to make each of these triangles inside them. Use a ruler.

1 isosceles triangle   **2** equilateral triangle    **3** scalene triangle    **4** right-angled triangle

Answer these questions.

5 What is the size of each angle in an equilateral triangle?

$\square$°

6 Can an isosceles triangle also be a right-angled triangle? Circle the answer.

Yes   No

6

Quadrilaterals

These diagrams show the diagonals of three quadrilaterals. Write the name of each quadrilateral.

1   **2**   **3**

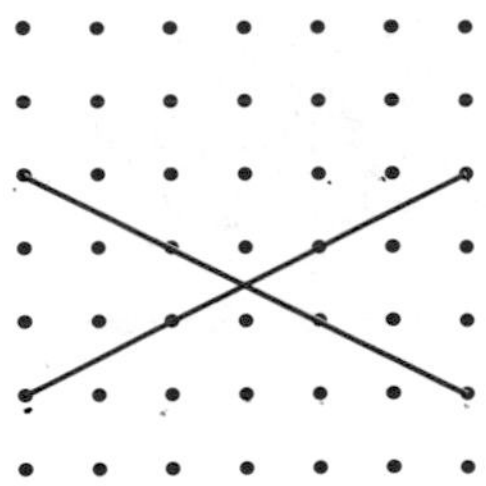

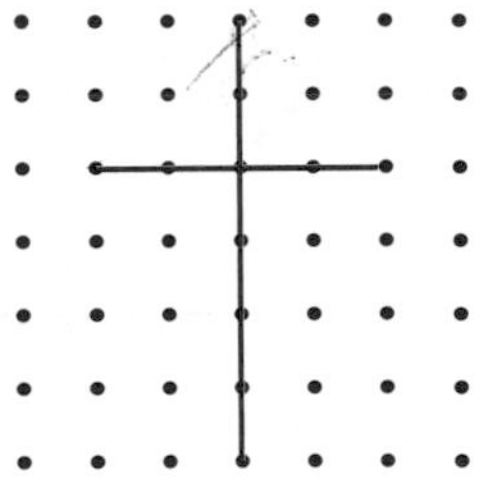

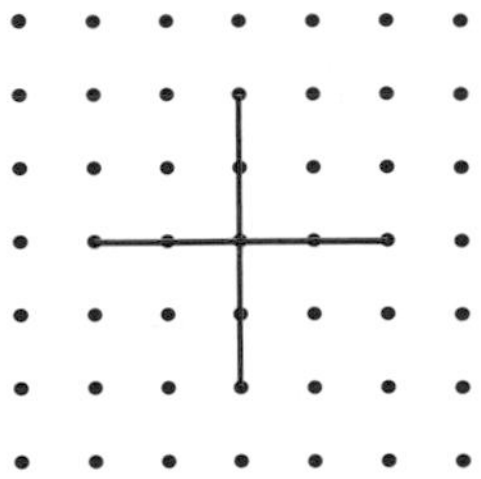

_____   _____   _____

For each statement tick (✔) True or False.

		True	False
4	A trapezium always has a pair of parallel lines.	☐	☐
5	A rectangle always has 4 equal sides and 4 right angles.	☐	☐
6	A kite sometimes has a right angle.	☐	☐

6

TOTAL MARKS 12

41

PRACTISE UNDERSTANDING SHAPE

3D shapes

Properties of 3D shapes

Solid shapes are 3-dimensional. Learn the names and properties of these 3D shapes.

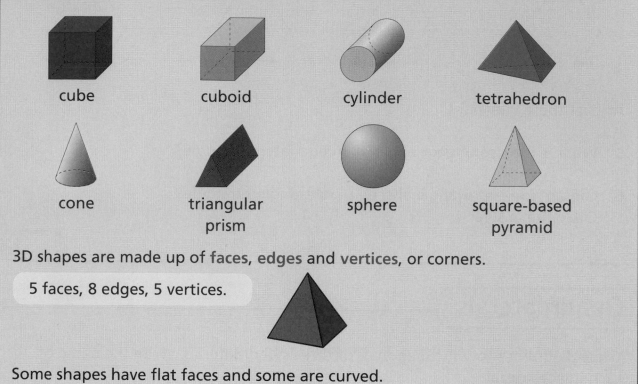

cube   cuboid   cylinder   tetrahedron

cone   triangular prism   sphere   square-based pyramid

3D shapes are made up of **faces**, **edges** and **vertices**, or corners.

5 faces, 8 edges, 5 vertices.

Some shapes have flat faces and some are curved.

2 flat faces, 1 curved face, 2 curved edges, 0 vertices.

Nets of solids

The **net** of a shape is what it looks like when it is opened out flat. If you carefully pull open a cereal box so that it is one large piece of cardboard – this is the net of the box.

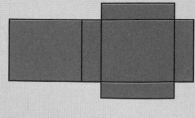

Net of a cuboid

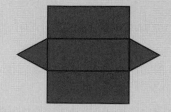

Net of a triangular prism

LEARN

UNDERSTANDING SHAPE

Properties of 3D shapes

Write in the properties of each shape to complete this table.

Shape		Number of flat faces	Number of vertices	Number of edges
Sphere		2	0	0
Cuboid		6	8	
Triangular prism			6	
Tetrahedron		4		
Cylinder				2
Square-based pyramid			5	

12

Nets of solids

Here is a net of a cube with no top.

1   Put a tick (✔) on the square which is its base.

2   Shade an extra square to make the net of a cube that does have a top.

Look at these nets of 3D shapes.

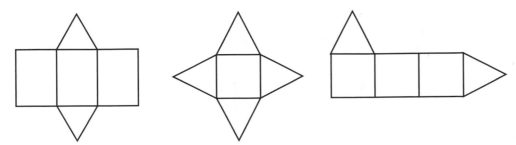

3   Colour red the net that will make a triangular prism.

4   Colour blue the net that will make a square-based pyramid.

4

TOTAL MARKS   16

Coordinates

Positions on a grid

Coordinates are used to show an exact position of a point on a grid.

Two numbers, one from the x axis and one from the y axis, show the position.

> The coordinates of A are (2,5).
>
> The coordinates of B are (4,3).

Coordinates are always written in brackets and separated by a comma.

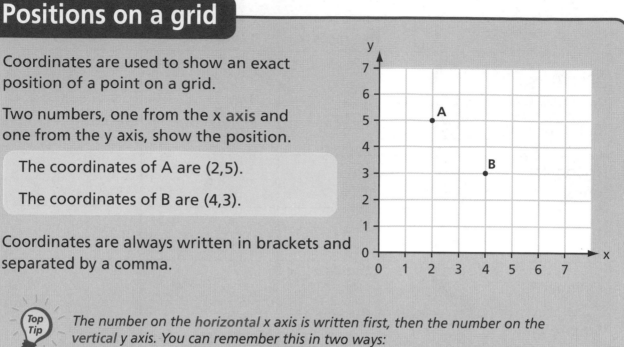

Top Tip

The number on the horizontal x axis is written first, then the number on the vertical y axis. You can remember this in two ways:
- *because x comes before y in the alphabet*
- *x is 'a cross': across!*

Shapes and coordinates

Coordinates are very useful for plotting the vertices of shapes.

> The grid below shows two sides of a square.
>
> What are the coordinates of the three vertices?
>
> Mark the missing coordinates for the fourth vertex and complete the square.

Remember to read the numbers across and then up for each position.

Draw in the missing lines, using a ruler to make it as accurate as possible.

The missing coordinates for the fourth vertex are (3,5).

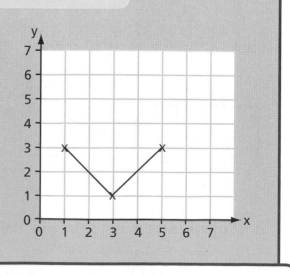

Key words   axis   horizontal   vertical

Positions on a grid

The tractor has coordinates (7,6).
Answer these questions.

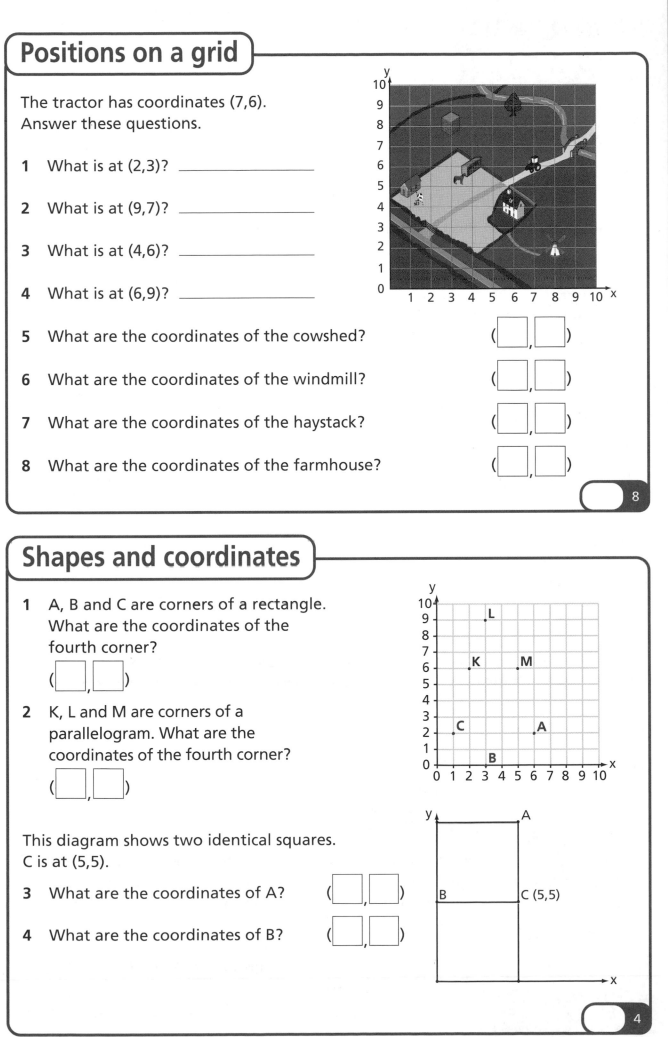

1   What is at (2,3)? _____

2   What is at (9,7)? _____

3   What is at (4,6)? _____

4   What is at (6,9)? _____

5   What are the coordinates of the cowshed?   (☐ , ☐)

6   What are the coordinates of the windmill?   (☐ , ☐)

7   What are the coordinates of the haystack?   (☐ , ☐)

8   What are the coordinates of the farmhouse?   (☐ , ☐)

8

Shapes and coordinates

1   A, B and C are corners of a rectangle.
    What are the coordinates of the
    fourth corner?

    (☐ , ☐)

2   K, L and M are corners of a
    parallelogram. What are the
    coordinates of the fourth corner?

    (☐ , ☐)

This diagram shows two identical squares.
C is at (5,5).

3   What are the coordinates of A?   (☐ , ☐)

4   What are the coordinates of B?   (☐ , ☐)

4

TOTAL MARKS   12

Angles

Types of angles

An angle is a measure of turn between two lines. Angles are measured in degrees (°).

There are 360° in a full circle.

These are special angles to remember:

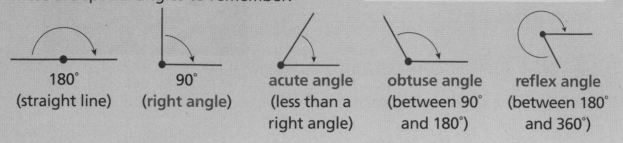

| 180° (straight line) | 90° (right angle) | acute angle (less than a right angle) | obtuse angle (between 90° and 180°) | reflex angle (between 180° and 360°) |

Measuring angles

A protractor is used to measure the size of an angle. It is a good idea to estimate the angle first and then measure it.

Read from the 0° on the scale.

Place the cross at the point of the angle you are measuring.

This angle is 45°.

Top Tip *Make sure you put the 0° at the start position and read from the correct scale. If you estimate the angle first, it will give you a good idea of the scale you should be reading.*

Angles and shapes

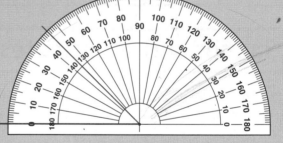

All the angles of a triangle add up to 180°.

$$a + b + c = 180°$$

All the angles of a quadrilateral add up to 360°.

$$a + b + c + d = 360°$$

To find the value of a missing angle on a triangle, find the total of the angles given and take it away from 180°.

$$35° + 90° = 125° \quad 180° - 125° = 55°$$

The missing angle is 55°.

Key words   right angle   acute angle   obtuse angle   reflex angle

The shapes below relate to all questions on this page.

A   B   C   D

Types of angles

Write in how many of each angle these shapes have to complete the chart.

Number of:	right angles	obtuse angles	acute angles	reflex angles
Shape A	2			
Shape B				
Shape C				
Shape D				

4

Measuring angles

Use a protractor and measure the angle marked x in each of the shapes above.

1   Shape A   angle x = [   ]°

2   Shape B   angle x = [   ]°

3   Shape C   angle x = [   ]°

4   Shape D   angle x = [   ]°

4

Angles and shapes

Without using a calculator, look at Shapes A–D and answer these. You have already measured angle x on each shape.

1   What is the size of the smallest angle on shape A?   [   ]°

2   What is the size of the smallest angle on shape B?   [   ]°

3   Shape C is an isosceles triangle. Calculate the size of one of the two equal angles.   [   ]°

4   Each of the two equal angles on Shape D is 30°. Calculate the size of the smallest angle.   [   ]°

4

TOTAL MARKS   12

Measures

Units of measure

Length, weight (or mass) and capacity are all measured using different units.

Length	Weight
1 centimetre (cm) = 10 millimetres (mm)	1 kilogram (kg) = 1000 grams (g)
1 metre (m) = 100 centimetres (cm)	Capacity
1 kilometre (km) = 1000 metres (m)	1 litre (*l*) = 1000 millilitres (ml)

It is important to write the units in your answers. For example, there is a big difference between 100g and 100kg!

Converting units

Once you know these **equivalent** measures, then you can convert from one unit to another. This always means multiplying or dividing by 10, 100 or 1000, depending on what you are converting.

This bookcase is 1.35m or 135cm high.

This bottle holds 2.25 litres or 2250 millilitres.

This pumpkin weighs 6.84kg or 6840g.

Reading scales

A scale is the marking of lines to help us measure, e.g. up the side of a jug, on weighing scales or on a ruler. You need to read scales carefully, using these steps:

1 Look at the unit – is it ml, cm, mm, g ..?

2 If it is level with a number, read off that number.

3 If it is between numbers, work out what each mark means and count on or back.

4 Remember to include cm, mm, g or whatever in the answer.

Key words   equivalent

Units of measure

Write each set of measures in size order, starting with the smallest.

1   1.8 litres   180ml   18 litres   80ml   _____

2   30mm   3.5cm   3.5mm   350cm   _____

3   $\frac{1}{2}$ kg   250g   50g   1.2kg   _____

4   60 litres   6600ml   600ml   6 litres   _____

4

Converting units

1   A recipe for soup needs 1 litre of water. 600ml is poured in.
    How much more is needed?   _____

2   A 2m length of wood is too long by 25cm. What is the exact
    length of wood that is needed?   _____

3   A jug holds $\frac{1}{2}$ litre of water. How many full jugs will it take to
    fill a 5-litre bucket?   _____

4   Noel is 1.35m. His younger brother David is 40cm shorter
    than Noel. What height is David?   _____

4

Reading scales

1   Which jug contains more
    water, Jug **A** or Jug **B**?   _____

2   All the water in these two containers is to be poured into
    an empty jug. How much water will there be altogether?   _____

3   What is the weight of the flour on Scale **A**?   _____

4   Scale **B** contains exactly the same
    amount of flour as Scale **A**. Draw
    an arrow on Scale **B** to the same
    weight as Scale **A**.

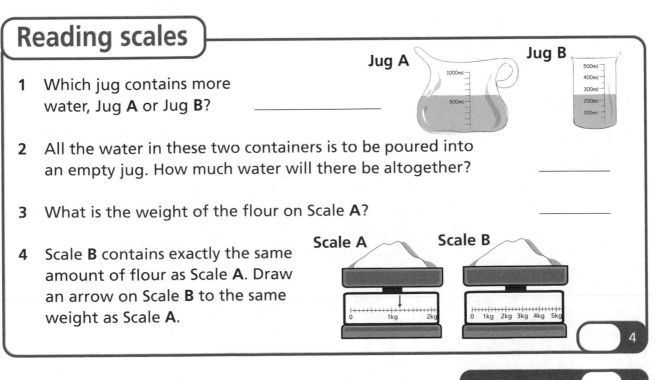

4

TOTAL MARKS   12

Perimeter and area

Perimeter of rectangles

The perimeter of a shape is simply the distance all the way around the edge.

The perimeter of rectangles can be found by totalling the length and width and then multiplying this by 2. Here is a formula for this:

2(length + width) or 2(l+w)

Perimeter = 2 (6.5 + 5) = 2 × 11.5 = 23cm

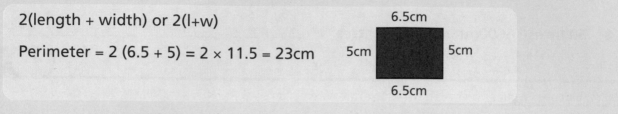

6.5cm

5cm   5cm

6.5cm

Finding areas

The area of a shape is the amount of surface that it covers. You can often measure the area of shapes by counting squares.

These shapes both have an area of 8 squares.

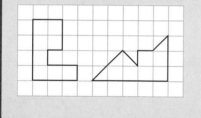

If the shape is not made up from whole squares, count all the squares that are bigger than a half.

This shape has an area of approximately 12 squares.

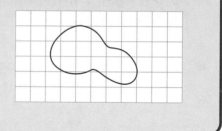

Area of rectangles

Finding the area of a rectangle is easy if you know the length and width.

The area is length x width.

Area = 3cm x 5cm = 15cm^2

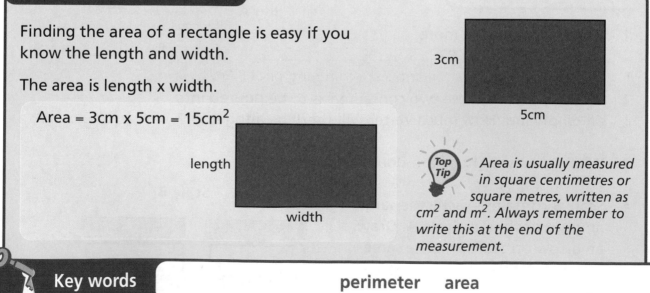

length

width

3cm

5cm

Top Tip Area is usually measured in square centimetres or square metres, written as cm^2 and m^2. Always remember to write this at the end of the measurement.

Key words   perimeter   area

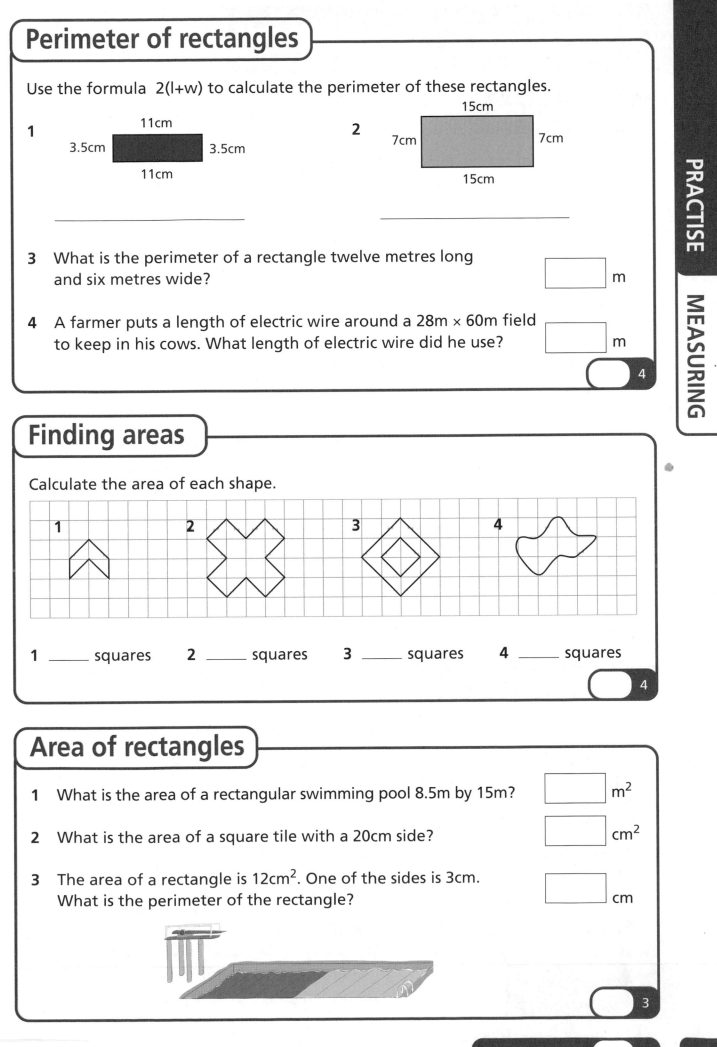

Perimeter of rectangles

Use the formula 2(l+w) to calculate the perimeter of these rectangles.

1   11cm
3.5cm   3.5cm
         11cm

2   15cm
7cm   7cm
             15cm

_____   _____

3   What is the perimeter of a rectangle twelve metres long
and six metres wide?   [   ] m

4   A farmer puts a length of electric wire around a 28m × 60m field
to keep in his cows. What length of electric wire did he use?   [   ] m

4

Finding areas

Calculate the area of each shape.

1   **2**   **3**   **4**

1 _____ squares   **2** _____ squares   **3** _____ squares   **4** _____ squares

4

Area of rectangles

1   What is the area of a rectangular swimming pool 8.5m by 15m?   [   ] m²

2   What is the area of a square tile with a 20cm side?   [   ] cm²

3   The area of a rectangle is 12cm². One of the sides is 3cm.
What is the perimeter of the rectangle?   [   ] cm

3

TOTAL MARKS   [   ] 11

Reading the time

24-hour time

We read the time using an **analogue clock** (circular) or **digital clock** (time in numbers). Digital clocks can be 12-hour or 24-hour clocks.

Timetables and digital watches often use the 24-hour clock.

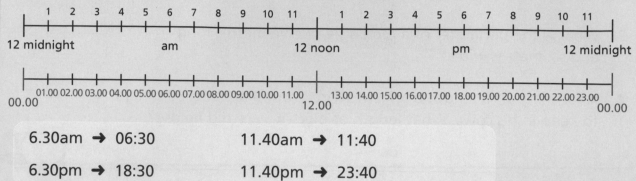

6.30am ➜ 06:30	11.40am ➜ 11:40
6.30pm ➜ 18:30	11.40pm ➜ 23:40

Morning (am) times look the same when you use 24-hour time.

For afternoon and evening (pm) times, you add 12 hours to find the 24-hour time.

You always use 4 numbers when you write the 24-hour clock, even for morning times.
So 9.45am is 09:45.

Top Tip **am** stands for ante meridiem and means before midday – from 12 midnight to 12 noon.
pm stands for post meridiem and means after midday – from 12 noon to 12 midnight.

Calculating times

To work out how long an event lasts, try counting on from the start to the finish.

A film starts at 6.40pm and finishes at 8.15pm.
How long does the film last?

Use a time line and count on.

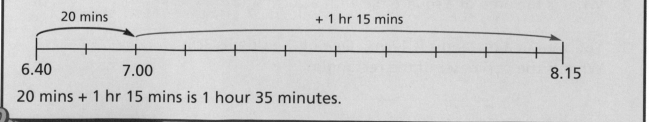

20 mins + 1 hr 15 mins is 1 hour 35 minutes.

Key words   analogue clock   digital clock
ante meridiem (am)   post meridiem (pm)

24-hour time

Draw a line to join six pairs of matching times.

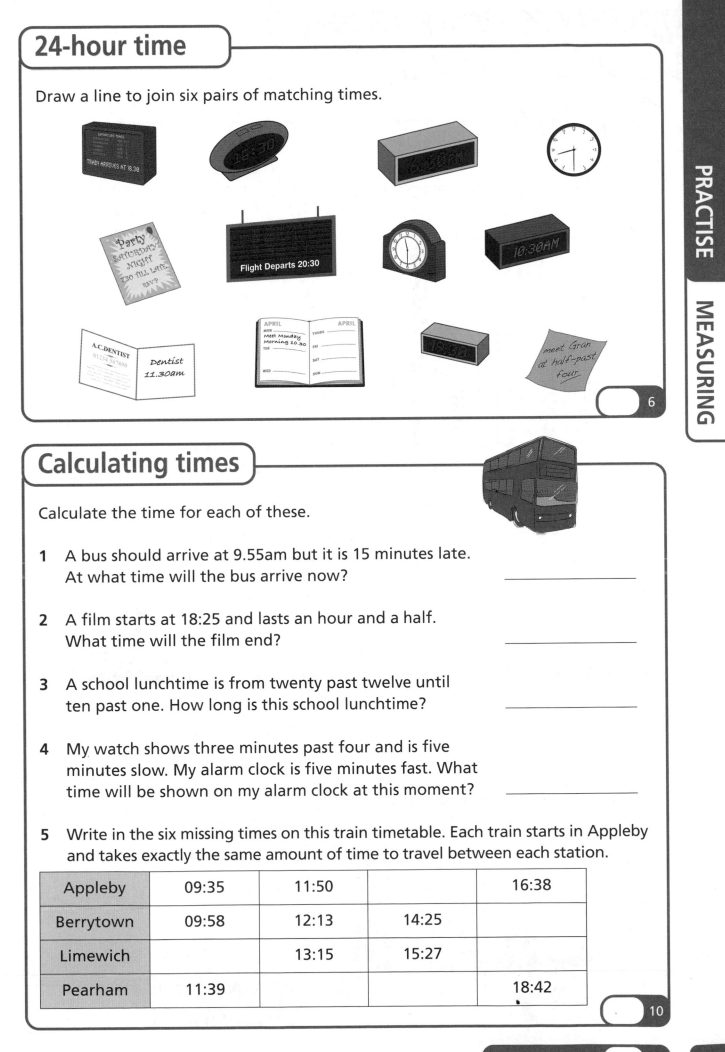

6

Calculating times

Calculate the time for each of these.

1   A bus should arrive at 9.55am but it is 15 minutes late.
    At what time will the bus arrive now?   _____

2   A film starts at 18:25 and lasts an hour and a half.
    What time will the film end?   _____

3   A school lunchtime is from twenty past twelve until
    ten past one. How long is this school lunchtime?   _____

4   My watch shows three minutes past four and is five
    minutes slow. My alarm clock is five minutes fast. What
    time will be shown on my alarm clock at this moment?   _____

5   Write in the six missing times on this train timetable. Each train starts in Appleby
    and takes exactly the same amount of time to travel between each station.

Appleby	09:35	11:50		16:38
Berrytown	09:58	12:13	14:25	
Limewich		13:15	15:27	
Pearham	11:39			18:42

10

TOTAL MARKS   16

Handling data

Bar charts

Bar charts are a useful way of showing information. To understand bar charts and other types of graph, look carefully at the different parts of the graph.

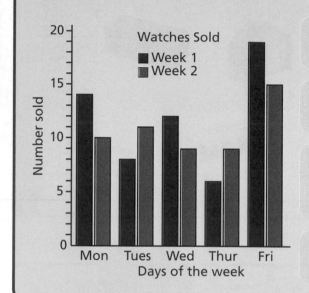

1 Read the title – what is it all about? Is there any other information given?

2 Look at the **axis** labels – these should explain the lines that go up and across.

3 Work out the scale – look carefully at the numbers – do they go up in 1s, 5s, 10s ..?

4 Compare the bars – read them across to work out the amounts.

Frequency charts and grouped data

The word frequency means 'how many', so a frequency chart is a record of how many there are in a group.

A teacher wanted to compare the number of laps of the playing field walked by a class of children on a sponsored walk. Here is the table of results.

Laps completed	6–10	11–15	16–20	21–25	26–30
Number of children	2	7	17	18	25

This group data can then be shown on a graph:

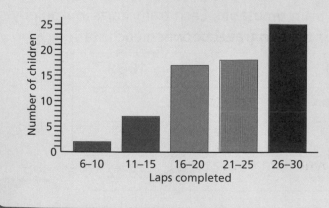

Key words   axis

Bar charts

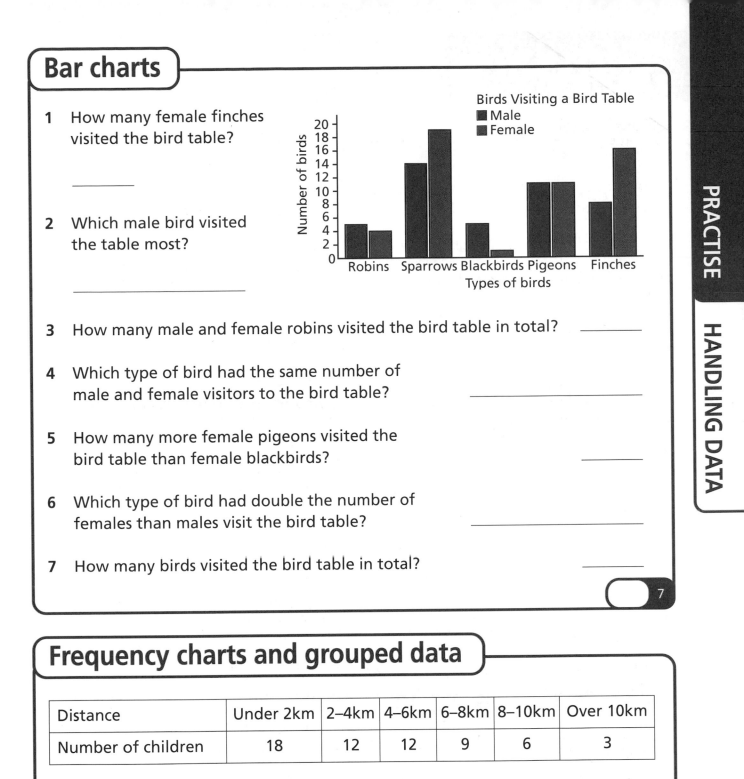

Birds Visiting a Bird Table
- Male
- Female

(y-axis: Number of birds, 0–20; x-axis: Types of birds — Robins, Sparrows, Blackbirds, Pigeons, Finches)

1 How many female finches visited the bird table?

_____

2 Which male bird visited the table most?

_____

3 How many male and female robins visited the bird table in total? _____

4 Which type of bird had the same number of male and female visitors to the bird table? _____

5 How many more female pigeons visited the bird table than female blackbirds? _____

6 Which type of bird had double the number of females than males visit the bird table? _____

7 How many birds visited the bird table in total? _____

7

Frequency charts and grouped data

Distance	Under 2km	2–4km	4–6km	6–8km	8–10km	Over 10km
Number of children	18	12	12	9	6	3

1 Which distance did the largest number of children travel? _____

2 How many children travelled a distance of 6–8km to school? _____

3 Half of the children travelling under 2km walk to school. How many children walk to school? _____

4 Kate travels 4.5km to school. Which distance group would she be included in? _____

5 How many children in total travel over 6km to school? _____

5

Glossary

acute angle an angle smaller than a right angle

adjacent near or next to something

analogue clock a round clock face with hands

ante meridiem (am) – past midnight and before midday

approximate a 'rough' answer – near to the real answer

area the area of a shape is the amount of surface that it covers

axis (plural is axes) the horizontal or vertical line on a graph

column a vertical arrangement of numbers, words or objects going up or down

decimal point a point that separates whole numbers from decimal fractions

denominator the bottom number of a fraction, the number of parts it is divided into. Example: $\frac{2}{3}$

difference the difference between two numbers is the amount that one number is greater than the other. The difference between 18 and 21 is 3

digit there are 10 digits, 0 1 2 3 4 5 6 7 8 and 9, that are used to make all the numbers we use

digital clock a clock with no hands that uses just numbers to show the time

divisor a divisor is a number that another number is divided by. Example: For $32 \div 4 = 8$, the divisor is 4

double make something twice as big, or multiply by 2

edge where two faces of a solid shape meet

equation where symbols or letters are used instead of numbers. Example: $3y = 12$, so $y = 4$

equivalent two numbers or measures are equivalent if they are the same or equal

equivalent fractions these are equal fractions. Example: $\frac{1}{2} = \frac{2}{4} = \frac{3}{6}$

estimate a good guess

face the flat sides of a solid shape

factor a number that will divide exactly into other numbers. Example: 5 is a factor of 20

formula a formula (plural is formulae) uses letters or words to give a rule

horizontal a horizontal line is a straight level line across, in the same direction as the horizon

improper fraction any fraction which is greater than 1, such as $\frac{5}{3}$, $\frac{8}{5}$ or $\frac{6}{2}$

mixed number any whole number and fraction written together, such as $2\frac{1}{2}$, $4\frac{3}{5}$ or $1\frac{3}{10}$

multiple a multiple is a number made by multiplying together two other numbers

net the net of a 3D shape is what it looks like when it is opened out flat

numerator the top number of a fraction. Example: $\frac{3}{5}$

obtuse angle an angle less than 180° (a straight line) but greater than 90° (a right angle)

parallel lines that are parallel always stay the same distance apart and never meet

percentage this is a fraction out of 100, shown with a % sign

perimeter the distance all the way around the edge of a shape or object

post meridiem (pm) – after midday or after noon

prime number only has two factors, 1 and itself. For example, 23 is a prime number as it can only be divided exactly by 1 and 23

proper fraction any fraction which is less than 1, such as $\frac{2}{3}$, $\frac{3}{5}$ or $\frac{1}{10}$

quotient this is the number of times that one number will divide into another number. Example: When you divide 18 by 3, the quotient is 6

reflex angle an angle between 180° (a straight line) and 360°

remainder if a number cannot be divided exactly by another number, then there is a whole number answer with an amount left over, called a remainder

right angle a quarter turn. The corner of a square is a right angle

sequence a list of numbers which usually have a pattern. They are often numbers written in order

square number numbers multiplied by themselves make square numbers. Example: $4 \times 4 = 16$. The first five square numbers are 1, 4, 9, 16 and 25

sum the sum of two or more numbers is the answer you get when you add them together

symmetrical when two halves of a shape or pattern are identical

vertical a line that is straight up or down, at right angles to a horizontal line

vertices (single is vertex) these are the corners of 3D shapes, where edges meet

Notes